STRENGTHENING FAMILIES

A Guide for State Policymaking

Judith K. Chynoweth
Barbara R. Dyer

Alice Tetelman, Executive Director
Alison Bishop, Production Manager

COUNCIL OF GOVERNORS' POLICY ADVISORS

Library of Congress Cataloging-in-Publication Data

Chynoweth, Judith K.
      Strengthening Families : a guide for state policymaking / by Judith K. Chynoweth,
      Barbara R. Dyer
             p. 112 cm.
      ISBN 0-934842-62-0
      1. Problem Families—Government Policy—United States. 2. Problem families—
      Services for—United States. 3. Problem children—Government policy—United States.
      4. Problem Children—Services for—United States. I. Dyer, Barbara R. II. Title.
      HV699.C48 1991
      362.82'8'0973—dc20   91-32535
                                                                  CIP

Cover Design by Market Sights, Inc.

Printed in the United States of America

The Council of Governors' Policy Advisors is a membership organization of the policy and planning
staff of the nation's governors. Through its office in Washington, D.C., the Council provides
assistance to states on a broad spectrum of policy matters. The Council also conducts policy and
technical research on both state and national issues. The Council has been affiliated with the
National Governors' Association since 1975.

Funding support for this publication was provided by a grant from the John D. and Catherine T.
MacArthur Foundation. The statements, findings, conclusions, recommendations, and other data in
this report are those of the authors and do not necessarily represent the views of the MacArthur
Foundation or the members of the Council of Governors' Policy Advisors.

Council of Governors' Policy Advisors
Hall of States
400 North Capitol Street, Suite 285
Washington, D.C. 20001
(202) 624-5386

Alice Tetelman
Executive Director

TABLE OF CONTENTS

ACKNOWLEDGMENTS

If there is wisdom in this guide, it is due to the diligence, counsel, and hard work of many to whom we are grateful. First, the ten governors and their teams who participated in CGPA's Policy Academy on Families and Children At Risk plowed the ground for much of what is in this guide. Through their leadership and tireless work, we were able to discover the elements critical to effective family policy. A special thanks to the team leaders who reviewed drafts and provided ideas and support along the way. They are Carol Rasco, Arkansas; Donna Chitwood and Barbara McDonnell, Colorado; Jess McDonald and Leo Smith, Illinois; Phillip Dunshee, Iowa; Nancy Grasmick, Maryland; Barbara Ross, Oregon; Joe Cocozza, Robert Frawley and Fred Meservey, New York; Ruth Vaughn Ford, Texas, and Sid Sidorowicz, Paul Trause, and John LeVeque, Washington. While the team members are too numerous to mention, each will see his or her hand in the development of this guide.

Those who served as coaches to the participating states contributed ideas and experiences and challenged our thinking. They are Steve Adams, Maine; Denise Alston of the Children's Defense Fund; Mary Alice Evans, Hawaii; Susan Karr, New Jersey; Robin Kimbrough, Nebraska; Rolanda Klapatch, Maine; Kathryn Seabolt, Georgia; Donna Spooner, Florida; Jerome Strong, Michigan; and L. Carl Volpe, Texas.

We owe a great deal to our colleagues and friends: Lauren Cook, who planted the seeds for the CGPA family project; Jack Brizius, Terry Buss, Mike Campbell, Bill Nothdurft, and Mark Popovich, whose ideas shaped ours on the family framework, assessment, accountability, and gaining support. We have also appreciated the opportunity to have learned from Charles Bruner, Judy Carter, Gail Christopher, Frank Farrow, Emily Fenechel, Rob Ivry, Janet Levy, Lisbeth Schorr, Tom Smith, Jerry Wishnow, and Nicholas Zill.

The academy was conducted in collaboration with the National Governors' Association (NGA), the American Public Welfare Association (APWA), and the Council of Chief State School Officers (CCSSO). We have gained a great deal from the experiences of our collaborators and, in particular, the efforts of Evelyn Ganzglass and Linda McCart of NGA, Richard Ferreira and Beverly Yannich of APWA, and Cindy Brown and Glenda Partee of CCSSO.

When this work was started, James M. Souby was Executive Director of CGPA. Now Alice Tetelman is at the helm. We are indebted to both for their encouragement and patience.

Were it not for the confidence and support of Pete Gerber, and the John D. and Catherine T. MacArthur Foundation, this guide would not be possible.

If you, the reader, find value in this work, thank those whom we have named. If you find fault, you have only us to blame.

1

PROLOGUE

ROSE is a child teetering on the
brink. Neither she nor anyone who
knows her can be certain whether
she will finish high school or drop
out, remain at home or run. In a
school composition, Rose wrote the
following:

*Right now it's only me and my little
sister that go to school. I really
want to graduate, but I doubt it if I
do. Graduating is my only hope. But
I am barely making it! I am trying
to, but it's hard, and that's life! All
my sisters and brothers are
dropouts, I see the way they are
right now, I wouldn't like to be like
them!*

Anyone who has spent a
little time with Rose would be
impressed by her intelligence,
sensitivity, and seriousness. She is a
warm, endearing girl, who cares
deeply for her family. Rose is in
trouble because her life is spinning
out of control, and she doesn't know
what to do about it.

Rose's recent history is
littered with corpses and broken
bodies. Three months ago, someone
shot her grandmother as she was
walking on the street. She is still in
the hospital. Two months before, her
uncle heard the sound of gunshots,
opened the door to his apartment,
and was riddled with buckshot. He
died a few hours later. "We all know

who hit him," Rose says. "They hang out in front of my house, but nobody will do anything about them."

In Rose's intimate circle, those who have not been shot or stabbed are wounded in other ways. On her way home from school, she often runs into her thirteen-year-old brother and his friends, who hang out in the alley a couple of blocks from where she lives. "Two years ago he was into grass and snorting spray paint. Last year it was acid and beer. But now he says they won't do anything for him. So he's using heroin. I see him every day in the alley passing the needle. He's always with the older men. They don't even try to hide it from me."

Her seventeen-year-old sister has two children. Although she has an apartment in a public housing project, she frequently visits Rose's parents.

"My mother and she fight all the time. My mother sees her life going down, but when she says something, my sister screams at her. With all the fighting and arguments, my mother gets all nervous. When my sister leaves, she starts to shake and cry. It's a little hard to concentrate on my homework in my house."

Rose sees young lives in decline all around her. One friend, a small, frail-looking child who just turned eleven, has had three miscarriages. Her closest friend recently left school to have a baby. Out of self-preservation, Rose has tried to distance herself from her sisters and the girls she grew up with. "I'm afraid I'll be like them," she says. But she worries, "My sisters and my friends are going to hate me because I don't hang with them. They think I'm acting like I'm too good for them. Yesterday there was a note in my school locker. Some girls said they were going to beat me up in the second lunch period."

Rose has compartmentalized her life. In school, aside from some difficulty with English and science, she gives the appearance of having her life in order. White blouse, blue pleated skirt, hair neatly cut in bangs, book bag slung over her shoulder—she could be any one of 2,000 kids in her school. Who could imagine what this tiny, slender girl, who giggles behind her palm, whose voice hardly rises above a whisper, has to endure every day after she leaves school? No one could imagine, because no one has bothered to find out. No teacher, no counselor, no principal knows Rose's life.[1]

RAY AND MAUREEN WASHINGTON married late in life. Ray didn't want to make the same mistake twice. When his first marriage went up in flames, he resolved to put all that was left of himself into raising his daughter Susan, and building his career. Maureen entered their lives when Susan was a young teenager. The adjustment was rocky at times, but Susan quickly found in Maureen the support her own mother had denied. Susan is now a freshman in college. Reflecting upon her tumultuous teens, she admits that she never would have made it without Maureen.

Ray and Maureen have a son, John, who is five years old. John has a disability and requires special attention; the only program available is in the next town over.

Ray's parents are both alive, although hardly living. His mother has Alzheimer's disease and slips in and out of lucidity, without warning. Ray's father is too frail to handle her, and the emotional strain is killing him. So Ray and Maureen have arranged for someone to come into the home each day to help out.

Maureen's father had a stroke six months ago and is living with them. The three months he spent in a nursing home nearly wiped him out financially.

Both Ray and Maureen work fulltime, but they claim to be barely staying above water. Between mortgage payments, Susan's tuition, after-school care for John, medical bills, groceries, and taxes, there isn't much left.

The stress has taken its toll on Ray. He is distracted at work, he has missed a few deadlines, and just isn't "on top of it" the way he used to be. His boss has little sympathy when Ray shows up late to work some mornings after dropping John off at school. He schedules meetings on those mornings without regard for Ray's needs.

"This isn't how I pictured it," says Maureen. "When I was young, I dreamed of working hard and getting ahead. But it seems that for every step forward, we're two steps behind. There isn't time to sleep, much less dream anymore."

INTRODUCTION

Families In Stress

Rose is not a pregnant teen, a school dropout, or a drug abuser. The Washingtons are not homeless, unemployed, or chronically ill. Neither family is found in case records or agency statistics, yet their chances of "making it" are in jeopardy.

The circumstances of Rose's life—her family, her neighborhood, her school—place Rose and her family squarely at risk of spiraling downward into long-term dependency.

The Washingtons are in a pressure cooker. They work relentlessly to come close to the middle-class standard of living their parents knew. But the stress of supporting children and aging parents, while keeping their fulltime jobs, could push them over the edge.

These two families are not alone. They are part of a growing number of families encountering problems so severe that their ability to sustain or improve their economic, health, and social conditions is threatened. One in four children is born poor, and a third of these children will spend part of their early years on welfare.[2] In 1988, more than 40,000 infants died before reaching the age of one year. Another 11,000 had low birth weights, placing them at greater risk of birth defects, learning disorders, and the need for long-term care.[3] Many of these infants are children of children. Young women in the United States under age fifteen are more likely to give birth than are adolescents in any other developed nation. Of the more than 488,000 teenagers who give birth each year, many are unmarried, poorly educated, and unprepared for child rearing.[4]

The structure and routine of American families is changing. Increasingly our families are middle-aged fathers and mothers caring for young children and aging parents. Parents, except teen parents, are having fewer children and are older when they do have children.[5] The elderly are growing in numbers and are living longer.[6] Also, more families are headed by a single adult. The number of single-parent families has increased from 3.8 million in 1970 to 9.7 million in 1990.[7] The United States has the highest divorce rate in the world. Over half of all marriages are expected to end in divorce. About 40 percent of America's children will experience the break-up of their parents before reaching age 18.[8] Children of divorced parents experience more emotional and behavioral problems and do less well in school.[9]

In two-parent families, the mother often contributes a significant portion of the family income, and the father plays a stronger role in parenting. Most children are still cared for by their parents. In dual-income households, schedules are juggled to accommodate work and child care responsibilities.[10] Increasingly, however, parents are relying on adults outside the home to provide child care. About 20 million children are cared for by an adult who is not a family member.[11]

The statistics on families are cause for alarm. Even more troubling is what they mask.

They don't reveal overlapping problems. While one family member may be unemployed and a substance abuser, another may be failing in school. An elderly member of the family may be suffering from a chronic illness while the youngest member is showing signs of a learning disability. Ray and Maureen care for aging parents, are putting one child through college, and have a young child with a learning disability. Ray is having problems at work. Maureen is showing early signs of depression.

The statistics also mask the progressive nature of these problems. A low birth-weight baby might experience developmental delays, enter school unprepared, exhibit aggressive behavior as a child, become pregnant as a teen, drop out of high school, become ill-equipped for the labor market, and remain unemployed. Ray could lose his job. Maureen could slip further into depression. What's more, people in the early stages of the progression frequently go unnoticed. Rose is not a statistic yet. A crisis or chronic problem has not yet forced her into the system.

Finally, the numbers don't show the connections among the individual, the family, and the neighborhood. Rose's neighborhood is rife with crime. Her peers do not respect her intentions to do well in school. She has no adult with whom to talk. The neighborhood is not a place where she and her family can feel safe, gain support for positive initiative, build confidence, or connect to the labor market.

Rose, Ray, and Maureen, and the stories of many families like these, reveal something that the data only hint at. It is the complex tangle of difficult life events, the characteristics of family members, and the perceived and real limits of support and opportunity present in the environment that place families at risk. This makes the problem tough to solve. Our systems are not yet geared to recognize or address clusters of interrelated problems. And the technology for dealing with multiple, intergenerational problems is still crude.

But the will is there. Many leaders at all levels are ready to change course. They know all too well that if families cannot provide their members with nurturing, safety, confidence, skills, and opportunities—and if neighborhoods not only fail to fill the gaps, but exaggerate them; we are all bound to pay the costs. The costs are increasing numbers of people who are ill-equipped for jobs and a steady deterioration of our economic and social foundation . . . escalating crime and an overburdened court and prison system . . . higher rates of catastrophic and chronic illness, and skyrocketing health care expenses. In the end, the greatest cost is the tragic loss of the nation's most valued resource—its people.

States Are Catalysts

Political leaders play a key role in changing social policy and public attitudes, and Governors are taking the initiative. During the last several years, Governors have spearheaded education reform, welfare reform, and comprehensive children and family initiatives across the nation.

The urgency to act now is heightened by the convergence of two forces— economic conditions and the passage of the Family Support Act of 1988.[12] More than half of the states are facing a decline in revenues. All are seeing costs for human services—health, welfare, education and criminal justice—rise dramatically.[13] The Family Support Act effectively changed the mission of state operated welfare systems from one of support to one that promotes self-sufficiency. States are grappling with the tasks of redefining their welfare policies and programs, as they explore less costly ways to achieve positive results across all categories of human investment.

In this climate, state policymakers are poised to reexamine their traditional roles as funder, provider of service, and regulator, and to develop or strengthen the following roles, which are less traditional:

The Governor as leader and catalyst. Governors are raising the family and children policy debate and calling for changes to promote cross-cutting initiatives and long-term investment at all levels of government.

The state as developer of new technology and information. State policymakers are devising better means for assessing the condition of families and children and understanding the underlying causes of problems. They are overcoming the limitations of existing data with new, more comprehensive systems, which focus on the long term and are oriented toward outcomes.

The state as enabler of families in partnership with cities and communities. State leaders recognize that the focus of their human investment should be to strengthen the ability of families to succeed. They also recognize that the best programs are community based. States are providing incentives for community-based initiatives and are engaging local governments, community leaders, and families in strategic policy development. They also are joining forces with local school boards, United Way and family service organizations, and business; and they are pooling investments with foundations and business groups.

The Challenge at Hand

State governments face a seemingly intractable problem: Regardless of the condition of a state's economy, substantial numbers of families continue to be at high risk of experiencing a host of interrelated problems such as long-term unemployment, poor health, teenage pregnancy, child abuse, inadequate housing, and drug addiction.

In response, states have attacked many of the symptoms and perceived causes of these problems. They have launched initiatives to prevent teenage pregnancy and school dropouts, to promote adult literacy and maternal and child health, to educate and train welfare recipients, and to enhance early childhood development.

Innovative and effective programs can be found for each of these problems. Why, then, do the problems of families and children seem to be growing worse? Why, with so much innovation sparked by state and local governments, do the institutions they command seem increasingly incapable of responding? While there is no single answer, there are several plausible explanations.

First, although the targets of these initiatives are often members of the same family, policies and programs have focused almost exclusively on service delivery to individuals—not on improved outcomes for families. Programs are designed to help individuals who fall into certain categories: teen mothers, illiterate adults, juvenile delinquents, displaced workers. These programs are funded categorically; they are regulated categorically; and their impacts are assessed categorically. The result has been an array of overlapping, loosely coordinated, and often costly initiatives addressing individual needs, but with little ability to strengthen entire families.

Second, little attention has been given to specifying the intended or desired outcomes of these efforts. Beyond a general intent to improve schools, decrease teenage pregnancies, and increase access to preventive health care, our systems—or even discrete programs—have remained unaccountable for solid, outcome-based performance. Reporting mechanisms that do exist focus almost exclusively on the process of providing services, not on the results of services.

Almost as damaging, the current system limits the way policymakers think about social problems and their solutions. When confronted by a problem, such as homelessness or drug abuse, policymakers are provided little information regarding the underlying causes, the connections between various symptoms, or how these problems are manifested in a family setting. Consequently, they move quickly to define the problem narrowly and to propose solutions that can be implemented within the structure of the current service delivery system. The typical response is to initiate a new categorical program and assign responsibility for it to a lead agency. This approach tends to perpetuate fragmentation in the delivery of services to people at risk.

Adding further complication is the fact that families have changed. There are more women in the work force, fewer mothers at home, more single-parent households, and more families caring for infirm, elderly relatives. Middleclass families are also under stress. Our human service policies address only a segment of families in trouble.

In summary, a major reason program innovations have not had widespread effect is that they are imbedded in systems that are increasingly dysfunctional. A history of excessive categorization; elaborate data systems that reveal little about real problems, underlying causes, or the results of actions; and funding and regulatory structures that reward processes—and not people—has made existing systems almost incapable of responding to the urgent needs of children and families. This policy guide is intended to help leaders turn this pattern around on behalf of children and families.

The Policy Guide

This policy guide for Governors and other public leaders offers a practical approach to designing policy—one that permits the welfare of families and children and helps them to achieve positive results. The guide is based on the direct experience of ten states that have developed comprehensive family initiatives through the Council of Governors' Policy Advisors (CGPA) Policy Academy on Families and Children At Risk. The chapters are organized according to the steps in the policy academy process. Figure 1 depicts these steps as a cycle.

Figure 1 *A Policy Cycle*

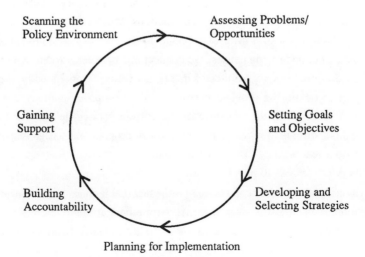

Chapter One presents a way of thinking about families in a policymaking context. Before initiating policy development on any complex, cross-cutting issue, it is important for policymakers to agree on some basic issues. Chapter One addresses these key questions:

- What do we mean by "family" and what do families do?
- What sorts of problems do families experience?
- Why do some families experience problems while others do not?
- How should government respond to family problems?

Chapter Two offers an approach to documenting and assessing the problems confronting families and children. The chapter identifies questions that Governors and their staffs must answer once they decide to develop a family policy. These questions range from "How many families do we have in our state with what sorts of strengths and problems?" to "What are the underlying causes of their problems, and how well are we dealing with them now?"

Chapter Three offers guidance on selecting goals and objectives for state family policy. Policymakers should begin by considering what would be different if the problem were solved. What constitutes success? What does it look like for people and for the systems that support them? The chapter begins with a hypothetical "happy ending" for two families. It then shows how this ending translates into specific and measurable, outcome-oriented objectives for both families and the systems that serve them.

Chapter Four focuses on developing and selecting strategies for family policy. While examples are drawn from states that have participated in CGPA's policy academy on families, the chapter is not a list of "what works." Rather, we argue that each state must develop its own unique mix of existing programs and innovative strategies based on a few guiding principles. The chapter closes with a brief discussion of implementation planning.

Chapters Five and Six present two critical components of implementation: building accountability systems and gaining support. Chapter Five discusses why creativity and innovation are not enough. Policymakers must develop accountability systems that enable them to monitor success and make course corrections over time. The questions of who must be involved in the development and implementation of family policy, and how and when, are tackled in Chapter Six. The process of gaining support is more than an initial stakeholder analysis, a legislative strategy, a Governor's speech, or a few public service announcements. Chapter Six ties these elements together into a marketing approach.

In Conclusion

Strengthening American families is not a matter of mere intellectual interest to a handful of public policy buffs. The family is the principle mechanism by which our values, culture, knowledge and aspirations are conveyed through generations. The future of the nation can be told by the condition of families today. If our families are in trouble, our future is in peril.

Developing effective policies to strengthen families is not a matter of putting a few new programs into place, or adjusting the old ones. It begins with a positive, yet realistic image of who we are, why our families are important. In the middle is a system—public and private—which taps into family strengths and provides support flexibly and effectively. The result is families who nurture, teach, adapt, and build.

14

MICHAEL

Family fortunes ebb and flow. It is the stuff of literature and popular novels—from *King Lear* to *War and Remembrance*. All too often it is reflected on the front page of the daily news:

ROCKLIN KNIFING SUSPECT: SPORTS STAR, BUT A TROUBLED TEEN

Things have gone decidedly wrong for the big red-headed kid who sported a Chris Mullin haircut, loved to shoot hoops and could quote Scripture.

On the basketball court, Michael was a 6-foot-4, all-league high school star in 1988, secure, confident and at ease among his former peers in high school. Off the court, however, Michael's security began to unravel when the twenty-year-old uncharacteristically dropped out of church after the basketball season ended and left his adoptive home, parents and foster brothers.[14]

     The Sacramento Bee briefly relates the facts of Michael's story: in and out of foster homes as a small child; successfully placed at age ten in a group foster home where he was eventually adopted; graduated high school as a sports star and active church member. Michael went on to community college, and his troubles started. His coach reported: "He was a sixteen-year-old kid in a big man's body who was having a hard time growing up. . . he didn't have the successes he had in the past." Michael quit sports. He was confused about his future. For a year he wandered from house to house, job to job. He visited his old high school coach looking for some answers: "Mike would say a lot of things. Mike had a lot of plans; most of them would fall through. He required a lot of pampering." In January 1990, Michael was held without bail for the attempted murder of a convenience store clerk.

CHAPTER ONE:
FOCUSING ON FAMILIES
AS A MATTER OF
POLICY

Understand What the Family Is, and What It Does

As the structure and routine of families undergoes change, so too must our definition of the family. Historically, we have relied upon a simple demographic description to define families—dual- or single-parent households. But given the many configurations of families and, more importantly, the need to know how well families are performing, a structural definition no longer suffices. We offer the following as a starting point:

> *A family is a group of people, related by blood or circumstances, who rely upon one another for security, sustenance, support, socialization, and stimulation.*

Gail Christopher, former director of the Family Development Institute in Chicago, argues that a family's job is to create responsible, self-sufficient adults through the provision of security, nurturing, socialization, education, self-esteem, validation, and comfort.[15] Families are strong when they perform these functions well. In the United States, most families can and do provide healthy and secure environments for their members.[16]

In all communities, however, there are families in turmoil, and all families have stressful moments. A first step in developing policies to strengthen the family is to recognize the important functions the family performs and the factors that influence its performance. In this book, we have organized the functions according to these broad categories: security, sustenance, support, socialization, and stimulation.

Security.

Security can be both physical and psychological. On the simplest level, it means a safe place to live—a home and community free from violence. Children and parents are free from abuse—physical, verbal, and emotional. On another level, security means a well-organized home with a comfortable routine, where members are safeguarded from accidents and chaotic events.

Sustenance.

To sustain is to meet basic needs —food, clothing, warmth, and emotional support. Sustenance of children begins before they are born. When a pregnant woman takes care of her own health; eats well; avoids drugs, alcohol, and smoking; and seeks good medical care, she is sustaining her unborn child.

Support.

A family supports its members both monetarily and emotionally. The family income buys products and services that enable family members to progress beyond maintenance. Emotional support moves beyond basic comfort to validation and the promotion of self-esteem. Children are actively encouraged to grow, to learn from their mistakes, and to take pride in their own achievements and those of their family and culture.

Socialization.

The family mediates between its members and society. Parents help children understand what is expected of them in social groups, at child care settings or preschool, on the streets, at school, and at work. Families teach and reinforce language, behavior, and social skills. The family transmits values and culture. Finally, the family helps its members understand and embrace differences between themselves and other cultures.

Stimulation.

One of the earliest and most important family functions is to stimulate intellectual growth in infants. But promoting the learning of family members—

whether they are preschoolers, school-age children, or parents improving literacy skills or changing careers—is a life-long family function.

In a society as culturally diverse as ours, it is essential to realize that the ways in which families perform these functions vary considerably. Just as all families do not look alike, neither do they function alike. Support, both material and psychological, will look very different in Hispanic, Latino, African-American, and Chinese-American families. The yardstick must measure how well these families are able to perform their functions, not whether the performance is the same in each family.

When families fail to provide many of these functions, their members are likely to experience problems. When a mother fails to sustain her unborn child during pregnancy, her infant starts life at a disadvantage. As in the case of Michael, children who are raised in an insecure and unpredictable family environment often become victims as adults or victimize others. Children who do not learn how to respond and/or adjust to societal expectations may drop out of school or become chronically unemployed. As adults, they often end up in society's institutions. If they have children, they can unwittingly continue a cycle of alienation and despair. Parents without job skills or problem-solving skills have a hard time supporting and seeking help for themselves or their families. Finally, without stimulation, children cannot grow or develop, be ready for school, advance their basic skills, or experience the joy of teaching others.

A functional view of families is grounded in the reality of what the family does or does not do for its members. Such a viewpoint encourages policymakers to distinguish families by how well they perform, not by their demographic characteristics. It supports a developmental view of the family, noting changes in function over time. It leads naturally to a consideration of the underlying causes of family problems as well as the outcomes of poor functioning. Finally, it allows us to look at family strengths, not just deficits, in a multicultural environment.

Recognize the Complex Interplay of Family Structure, Characteristics, Conditions, and Circumstances that Influence Family Functioning

It is important to know how the structure of families is changing. More importantly, we need to better understand the relationship between how well a family functions and its structure.

Family Structure

The commonly accepted structural elements that make up a family include a single individual, a man or woman with children, a couple without children or with children of particular ages. The U.S. Census Bureau distinguishes between a household —all persons residing in a housing unit—and the more exclusive family unit—a group of two or more persons related by blood, marriage, or adoption, who reside together. It also distinguishes between family- and non-family households.[17]

A structural view of families highlights how families are changing. The New York State Council on Children and Families conclude in its report *The State of the Child*:

> *The traditional view of families—a married couple with children in which the father is the sole provider—is for most children a view of the past. Only 38 percent of all children in New York State lived in such a "traditional" family in 1980 compared with 54 percent in 1970. The rest lived in a wide variety of family configurations, including single-parent families, extended families, and cohabiting families.*[18]

Looking at structure alone has serious limitations, however. It does not distinguish between families that function well and those that function poorly. It gives no clue as to why certain families experience problems or why some families have the resources to overcome temporary setbacks. Looking at family characteristics, conditions, and circumstances, along with structure, helps to fill out the picture.

Descriptive Characteristics—Risk Factors and Strengths

Characteristics commonly attached to family members include age, ethnicity, welfare or employment status, employment history, and educational status. Family conditions and circumstances include income level, family composition, and community attributes. Statistically, certain individual and family characteristics, circumstances, and conditions are linked to particular outcomes.

When characteristics are statistically associated with negative outcomes, they are referred to as risk factors. Poverty, for example, is a powerful predictor of negative outcomes for family members, including poor academic performance, low educational status, poor health, teen pregnancy, and loss of self-sufficiency.

In addition, multiple risk factors increase the likelihood of negative outcomes. By focusing on whole families, policymakers can see more clearly the impact of multiple risk factors on individual family members.

In discussing the results of several studies of groups of children and animals over time, Lisbeth Schorr concluded:

> *These studies demonstrate that it takes more than a single risk factor to elicit an adverse outcome. They have rendered moot earlier controversies over nature versus nurture, by showing that the interplay between constitution and environment is far more decisive in shaping an individual than either alone.*[19]

Whether the studies are on rhesus monkeys, low birth-weight babies, babies with immature sleep organization, the children of Kauai, or delinquent youth, the evidence is the same. A single risk factor can often be overcome through individual adaptability or a nurturing environment. Multiple risk factors, especially the interaction of individual characteristics with environmental deprivation, tend to create lasting damage on children and their families.

Let's look at an example drawn from the literature on teen pregnancy. Louise Flick has identified four decision points related to adolescent parenthood: (1) the decision to become sexually active, (2) the decision not to use contraceptives, (3) the decision to carry the pregnancy to term, and (4) the decision to raise the child rather than give it up for adoption. Each decision point is associated with a number of factors. Flick has grouped them under several headings: demographic, family, individual, psychological, peer group, and couple relationship.[20]

Susan Foster summarized several of these factors in her policy guide, *Preventing Teen Pregnancy*:[21] Older teenagers are most likely to be sexually active if their educational status and the educational status of their parents and siblings is low. Younger teens are more likely to be sexually active if living in poverty. Metropolitan residence is also a factor, especially when combined with living in an area of concentrated poverty.

The following family characteristics have a positive association with teenage sexual activity: larger family size, single parent family, an older sibling who is a teen parent, low parental involvement, and poor parent-child communication. Individual factors include values, self-esteem, and expectations. High school students who value independence highly yet have low expectations for achievement are more likely than their peers to be sexually active. High self-esteem is associated with beginning sexual activity for males.

These factors are associated with just one decision point—to become sexually active. Going back to Rose, how many of the above characteristics do she and her family have? Policymakers cannot say for sure that Rose will become a teen mother. But if she does, they can draw the conclusion that the interaction of multiple risk factors was a major underlying cause.

Looking at risk factors only, however, has several disadvantages: First, it may target families by characteristic when in fact they do not need help. While certain characteristics are associated with negative outcomes, they do not guarantee negative outcomes. Many single mothers are able to raise their children in good health, graduate from high school or college, and be successfully employed.

Second, families that do not have the standard "at-risk profile" may not be recognized as needing help. Rose was not eligible for any program. While most people would think of Rose as being "at risk," she currently does not fit into any agency's definition of a person for whom services should be provided.

Third, the characteristics of the family may become confused with underlying causes, making it more difficult to solve the real problems confronting the family. For example, African-American and Hispanic children are more likely to drop out of school than are white children. Yet, careful statistical analysis of high school dropout predictors found that when socioeconomic factors are controlled, differences across racial, ethnic, and geographic lines blur.[22]

Linking ethnicity to negative outcomes can be especially pernicious and promote stereotyping. For example, African-American family culture is not the cause of rising numbers of births to young, unmarried black teenagers. The causes, as William Julius Wilson painstakingly points out in his book *The Truly Disadvantaged*, are complex and may relate more to young, black male unemployment than so-called cultural tradition.[23] Margaret Wilkerson and Jewell Handy Gresham decry the negative image of "teeming black female fecundity . . . and of feckless black males who abandon their children" when "the most critical problem relating to the plight of black unwed mothers is the massive unemployment of the males who would otherwise be potential mates for them."[24]

Fourth, risk-factor descriptions of families tend to be static. They do not capture how these characteristics change over time. For example, not all poor families are likely to remain so. Some families are poor because they are headed by someone who is physically or psychologically unable to work. Other families may be undergoing wrenching, temporary shocks—divorce, illness, death of a spouse, sudden unemployment. In still others, both parents work multiple, part-time jobs, hovering sometimes above, sometimes below the poverty line.

The fifth disadvantage to looking at risk factors only is that these factors by definition focus exclusively on weaknesses, not family strengths. Most descriptive definitions are driven by social research looking at factors associated with negative, rather than positive outcomes. Such descriptions promote isolation of at-risk families, they do not galvanize support for them.

While social science research provides considerable information on factors associated with failure, much less is known about family characteristics that promote healing, self-esteem, career advancement, and social progress. Fortunately, researchers are paying more attention to why some families and children succeed in spite of difficulties. Such "success factors" include the following:

Positive parental attachment.

Many studies, including those summarized by Lisbeth Schorr in *Within Our Reach*, have documented the importance of positive parental attachment for successful childhood development.[25] Though research on the benefits of parental attachment for older children is just emerging, it seems evident that a constellation of positive parental behaviors leads to greater well-being for both parent and child.[26]

Higher educational status.

Berlin and Sum discuss the relative advantage enjoyed by children of parents who are better educated. They cite the work of Thomas Sticht, Catherine Snow, and others, which shows that "parents who speak with their children, rather than at or past them, foster larger vocabularies and better language skills."[27] Recent research by Berlin and Sum found that higher grade level attainment in mothers was associated with higher grade level achievement in their children.[28]

Higher education achievement improves outcomes for the parents themselves. Frank Furstenberg, who followed 300 inner-city teenage mothers for seventeen years, found that "education was the most potent avenue for escape from poverty and welfare." Significantly, this fact held true even if the mother waited until her twenties or thirties to go back to school.[29] Berlin and Sum concluded that raising the mean of tested basic skills of young adults by only one grade equivalent would result in a dramatic improvement in outcomes: "lifetime earnings would increase by 3.6 percent, and the likelihood of births out of wedlock, welfare dependency, and arrests would decline by 6.5 percent, 5.3 percent, and 6.2 percent, respectively.''[30]

Employment.

Because low income and unemployment are strongly associated with many negative outcomes in health, education, and social behavior, we can conclude that employment is a condition that leads to more positive outcomes for families. As Jewelle Taylor Gibbs points out in her article on young black males and the new morbidity, the issue may not be absolute level of income but the relative deprivation perceived by young blacks where they live. Young black men who both have aspirations and see paths for achieving them are less likely to kill themselves or others, or engage in alcohol or drug abuse, or other risky, life-threatening behaviors.[31]

Self-Esteem.

Widespread belief supports the notion that high self-esteem leads to positive outcomes such as school achievement and completion. Yet, while social science literature speculates that low self-esteem is associated with negative outcomes, no studies have demonstrated conclusively that high self-esteem leads to positive outcomes. In fact, two researchers found that being popular is associated with teen fatherhood in minority youth. Their sample of male teens at risk of fatherhood was not low on powerlessness or self-esteem.[32] Berlin and Sum note that self-esteem and achievement are closely interrelated. It is difficult to tell which causes which.[33]

Positive Expectations.

The literature is not ambivalent about the relationship of negative expectations on outcomes. Low expectations result in self-fulfilling prophecy. Once again, however, few studies document the converse—that high expectations of children or their parents lead to positive outcomes. We know that respect and higher expectations are conveyed by giving students individual attention, accepting their feelings, monitoring their progress, and avoiding behaviors that create a negative climate in the classroom and in the school. But we are left to assume that conveying respect and positive expectations will lead to higher educational achievement and fewer social problems over the long run.[34] While countless autobiographies and anecdotes give testimony to the significant positive effect one caring adult can have on a young person's life, only a few studies document this.[35]

Opportunities.

Finally, where there is opportunity and choice in the family's environment, more positive outcomes are achieved. Studies in health care, nutrition and family planning services, and early childhood education bear this out. Choices need to be available for compensatory and alternative education programs and in school-to-employment transition programs.[36]

One can think about success factors in terms of the "three Cs." *Competence,* particularly in the form of educational achievement, leads to quality employment, which in turn fosters family functioning. It also leads to better educational achievement for one's children. *Confidence,* as imparted through the expectations of others and one's own achievements, leads to effort, commitment, and, frequently, success, promoting further confidence. *Connections,* to education and employment opportunities and to health and other services, promotes family functioning and supports the attainment of education and skills by family members.[37]

Policymakers cannot say for certain why families function the way they do. Some are drawn toward disaster while others triumph over circumstance. As social research generates new knowledge, the answers will become clearer. Meanwhile, policymakers must make choices on the basis of available information. They will be helped in this task by knowing how families are structured in their state, by reviewing the literature on risk factors, by considering the interaction of risk factors within their families, by recognizing that overreliance on risk factors can lead to serious policy mistakes, and by taking advantage of known factors that support family strengths.

View the Whole Family Over Time

In the mid-1980s, a series of longitudinal studies were conducted on welfare recipients in Michigan.[38] The analysis sent shock waves through the social policy community. The data on welfare households viewed over time painted a very different picture than those viewed from separate points in time. What looked like a somewhat uniform group of welfare families at fairly constant case load levels could be separated into at least three distinct groups when watched over time. One group received income assistance for a relatively short period of time. With little outside help, the head of household got a job and moved off the welfare roles. A second group of recipients seemed to move through a revolving door—off assistance after a short period of time, but then back on. A third group, a much smaller percentage of the whole than originally thought, consisted of those families chronically dependent (two years or longer) on welfare assistance. At about the same time, studies on the long-term, negative consequences of foster care for children were being published.[39] These studies, too, demonstrated the importance of observing families over time.

Going back to Michael's story at the beginning of this chapter, what is so troubling is that he and the many families that raised him were helped by government services, by community institutions, by the school, and by concerned adults. His story brings despair to the hearts of service providers and anger and frustration to the minds of taxpayers. One can imagine Michael as the state services system observed him—in snapshots: at five, the day he is removed from his home; at five and a half, six, and eight, in three different foster care settings; at thirteen, the day of his adoption; at eighteen, the day of his graduation. There, the picture taking stopped, though Michael's need did not. Somehow, when Michael was supposed to be ready to live on his own, he simply wasn't. Michael could not change inside as fast as his circumstances changed on the outside. Help was not there when he needed it.

The balance of negative factors and supports shifts in the life of a family and its members. The environment surrounding families also changes. Consider Rose's family. Their neighborhood deteriorated. Jobs and services disappeared, followed by a dramatic increase in drugs and street violence. Some families, perhaps the Washingtons, appear to have the resources to deal with negative conditions and changing circumstances. They have inner reserves of esteem, strength, and flexibility. They can marshall outside resources, seek help from others, understand and face their difficulties, make decisions, and move on. Others cannot.

Our examples illustrate several reasons why policymakers who wish to help families must observe them over time. First, such observation captures a more accurate picture of who needs help, when they need it, and why—all critical factors in tailoring services to strengthen family functioning. Some families—like those receiving welfare because of a temporary setback—may not need help at all. Others, like the Washingtons, may need a referral to temporary family respite care. Michael and his families may need occasional support over a long period of time. Another family, like Rose's, may benefit from intensive assistance on several fronts for a year or more.

Second, observing whole families over time presents a clearer picture of how early interventions can avert tragedy, even start the family back on the road to self-sufficiency. Through no fault or characteristic of her own, Rose is one step away from tragedy. A family policy grounded in an understanding of how a family changes over time could identify Rose early on, in her own community; assess the strengths, weaknesses, and needs of her entire family; and develop a family plan for addressing priority concerns *before* Rose followed in her sister's or brother's path of despair.

Third, data on families collected over time can document the costliness of helping at-risk families after situations have deteriorated, thus demonstrating the need for and cost-effectiveness of prevention or early, intensive intervention. Most likely, a total of the present and future estimated costs of services to Rose's entire family would be high. One could factor in the cost of the grandmother's health care, welfare costs for Rose's sister and her children, and drug treatment and possibly correctional system costs for her brother. This list does not include lost income and taxes from those who drop out of high school. The cost of providing foster care and related services to Michael and his families must have been high— not to mention the costs incurred during his involvement with the correctional system. Needless to say, this accounting does not factor in the human loss of so many young lives wasted.

Typically, government services view individuals at a single point in time. Programs focus on single individuals and problems. Other individual or family problems, however related they may be, are simply not considered relevant to eligibility determination or service design and delivery. Information on multiproblem families, as is further discussed in Chapter Two, is not captured by state data systems. Finally, due to large case loads, even caseworkers seldom follow entire families over time. These practices will have to change if policymakers wish to understand how families function and what will be most helpful to them.

Focus Attention on Family Outcomes

Policymakers are used to tracking services. A typical social services report documents the number of checks sent out, the number of available day care slots, the number of prenatal exams given, the amount of contracted counseling hours, and so forth. These reports say nothing about results. Are families self-sufficient? Are children in developmentally appropriate child care settings, and are they receiving adequate support and stimulation? Has the number of low birth-weight babies declined?

An outcome is an event or circumstance understood to be the result of a process or a chain of events. It is hoped that an outcome is the result of a successful policy intervention. But any particular outcome is never the end of the line. It is often the beginning of another chain of events resulting in further outcomes. Risk factors are outcomes that are associated with negative events or circumstances. Rose is a good example. If the circumstances of Rose's life do not improve, she will be further at risk of having a low birth-weight baby and becoming chronically unemployed or dependent on welfare. Her baby will then be at risk of chronic poverty and lower educational achievement, thus repeating the entire cycle.

Once policymakers begin to focus on families over time and observe how their characteristics and circumstances shift, outcomes no longer appear as a single point but as multiples on a continuum that progresses from negative to positive. Consider the families in the Michigan poverty studies. Each subgroup moved along an employment or self-sufficiency continuum that looked like this:

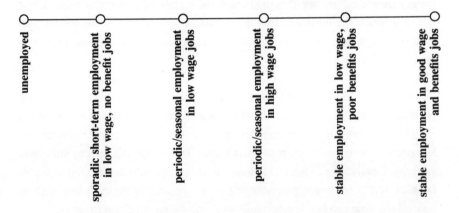

Envisioning family outcomes on a continuum offers several advantages to policymakers. First, it presents a more accurate picture of what happens to families and how they may differ from one another. Plotting individuals or families on an outcome continuum naturally leads to an exploration of the underlying reasons why some families fail to progress and others do not. This analysis of barriers enables policymakers to target appropriate interventions to those who need them. In fact, such an analysis contributed to the development of the Family Support Act, which provides selected services such as job readiness skills, day care, literacy training, or job training to those who need them to achieve steady employment at a given wage standard.

Second, arraying desired results on a continuum enables policymakers to set priorities in times of fiscal constraint. It may be more important to ensure basic levels of health through preventive health services to women and young children than to subsidize costly organ transplants. It may be more desirable to support intensive, integrated services to families at risk of chronic welfare dependency than to fund short-term training for low-wage jobs. While arraying short-term policy trade-offs, the continuum maintains a clear focus on long-term positive outcomes for all families: healthy lifestyles/positive health status and stable employment/good wages and benefits.

Finally, plotting families on an outcome continuum may improve our understanding of how situations deteriorate over time, strengthening our ability to determine early warning signals for intervention. Let's return to Michael. He was moving successfully along the education continuum until he hit a snag. His downward slide was visible to family members, his coaches, and his friends. He quit basketball; he quit school; he moved from job to job. Unfortunately for him and for the convenience store clerk, intervention came too late—on the 911 line.

So far in this chapter, we have encouraged policymakers to understand what the family is and what it does. In particular, we have stressed the value of using a functional definition of the family and of recognizing how the complex interplay of family structure, characteristics, and circumstances influence family functioning. We have urged the policymaker to view the whole family over time and to focus attention on family outcomes. Our final point: Recognize that improving outcomes for families will take time and significant change in state systems. Plan for this.

Take Action Over Time

In *Within Our Reach*, Lisbeth Schorr lays out the full menu of what we know works to improve outcomes for children. She is not alone in saying that we have enough knowledge to take action. Wilson, Gibbs, Berlin, Sum, Hahn, Danzberger, and Lefkowitz[40] among many others, elegantly summarize a veritable banquet of effective actions. Not knowing what works is not the difficulty. Understanding how to take persistent, effective action over time in a political environment is.

Our culture has a "fix-it" mentality; but governments cannot fix families. They can help families learn to help themselves. This is a process that takes place over time, and there are many possible points of intervention. Policymakers should see their interventions as points along the path of family growth and development.

Review again our picture of the family over time (Figure 2). Imagine Rose and her family in this chart. Rose's family lives in an environment that offers few opportunities and many negative influences. This combination of risk factors accumulating over time has almost drowned Rose. Yet the family continues to have some strengths. Rose is intelligent; she still has hope; she is still in school. Her mother cares for her daughters and tries to communicate with them.

Effective interventions to help Rose and her family are available. An isolated intervention at one point in time—a counseling session for Rose with the school counselor, a thirty-day treatment program for Rose's brother, a ninety-day work-training program for Rose's mother—may not be able to reverse the downward trend of this family. But a series of planned interventions—intensive and well coordinated, conducted with the family's involvement—will certainly help Rose's family.

Figure 2 *The Family Over Time*

The Environment

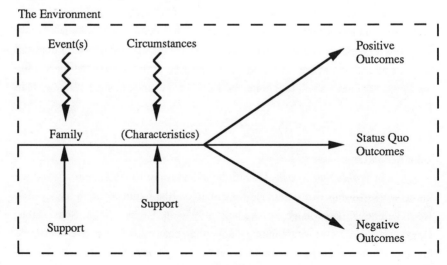

Although such interventions are available, affordable systems for state-wide, broad-scale delivery of integrated interventions are not. This is the policy challenge for those who wish to help families. Earlier interventions require less expenditure of energy and resources to move the family toward more positive outcomes. Schorr reminds us that effective intervention for only one risk factor—employment, early childhood education, parent education, quality health care—can have positive results for an entire family system:

> *As we have seen, no one circumstance, no single event, is the cause of a rotten outcome. School failure, delinquency, teenage pregnancy—none is dependent on a single devastating risk factor. But each risk factor vanquished does enhance the odds of averting later serious damage. A healthy birth, a family helped to function even though one parent is depressed and the other seldom there, effective preparation for school entry—all powerfully tip the scales toward favorable outcomes.*[41]

Improving outcomes for Rose, Michael, and other families like theirs is within our reach. To succeed, policymakers must make a dedicated and persistent effort to change the systems that deliver services to families. It is not a question of designing a new program, creating a new target group, or implementing a two-year initiative. Instead, it will take long-term commitment to informed decision making; collaborative policy development; and new approaches to program planning, funding, contracting and services delivery at the local level. State policymakers will encounter difficulties in meeting this challenge. The policy framework presented in this chapter is one tool that can help. State policymakers may wish to refine this framework. We encourage you to make it your own. We are confident that your attempts to define the family policy territory will guide your initial steps in the challenging task of helping families help themselves.

The next several chapters explore the major challenges that face policymakers who want to take action in this area and offer suggestions on how to overcome them. Chapter Two discusses the limitations on information that policymakers confront in assessing family problems in their state.

THE NEW GOVERNOR had become acutely aware of the Roses, Michaels, Rays and Maureens in the state when, in her prior position as a corporate chief executive officer, she chaired the state business roundtable task force on education reform. The largest city in the state had a 35 percent school dropout rate. The roundtable task force conducted a series of hearings and site visits, and reviewed agency reports in that city. As a result of that experience, the Governor became convinced that improving schools, while essential, isn't enough. Strengthening families is central to success.

Throughout her campaign she emphasized her commitment to families. Her stump speeches captured the crowd with images of healthy babies, vibrant schools, skilled workers, work environments that support modern-day families, and economic prosperity. She was determined to see that all families' basic needs were met and that each had the chance to be a full participant in the wealth of opportunities available in the state. Her proposed path was to convert the faceless human services system into a community of "people helping people." She called for a system that takes its lead from families, responding to needs and building on strengths.

Now in office, harsh reality takes hold. The state is choked by recession. Revenues are shrinking and costs are escalating. Both Aid for Dependent Children (AFDC) caseloads and confirmed child abuse reports are up. Drug and crime problems play in major urban newspapers every day. Health, education, and crime account for two-thirds of the state budget already, and the cost of new federal Medicaid mandates are beginning to squeeze out everything else.

The Governor calls in her key advisors: the director of policy and his senior human resource analyst; her press secretary and political advisor; the heads of the departments of health, human services, corrections, labor, economic development, and education; and the head of the education/business coalition. She turns to the group and says:

I stand firm on my commitment. My top priority as Governor is to aggressively attack the problems confronting so many families in our state. I want us to work as a team to get this job done. These issues cut across all of your departments. I want to propose an initiative by the next legislative session. But first, we need to know more.

We spend over half of our budget on families and children and yet the situation deteriorates. I want details on who our families are; how well they are functioning; which ones are doing well, which are in trouble, and why; how well they are served, by whom, and at what cost.

The policy team begins work on an assessment, pulling information from each of the agencies and a number of other sources. Where they cannot find data, they conduct their own surveys and hold focus groups. Two months later, they meet again with the Governor. The policy director pulls out several charts:

Most families who have problems manage to improve their situation within a year. Some receive help from our programs, and many rely on their own strengths, resourcefulness, and support from their extended family and community members.
This chart reflects the typical families we serve in our welfare, mental health, and at-risk education programs. The first type of family comes into our system with
only one or two problems—the most common are unemployment and poor basic education or job-readiness skills. Our data show that this type of family—about 65 percent of our sample—receives help for about six to twelve months. We also know that this type of family exhibits many strengths, ranging from parental involvement in school to consistent health maintenance.

The second type of family has multiple problems. You can see from this chart how negative outcomes for parents — alcohol and drug abuse—interact with negative outcomes for their children, such as learning disabilities and abuse and neglect. Multiproblem families represent about 25 percent of our AFDC case load, almost 85 percent of our child welfare case load, and about—this is a guess, Governor— 20 percent of children who are educationally at risk. These same families are receiving help from many of our programs for a period of two years or much longer. These families also exhibit important strengths. Parents have hopes for their children, family members are capable of withstanding enormous stress, and these people know how to access and work the system.

32

We can't remove these families from our caseloads, because we estimate that without intervention their situations would worsen and cost the state even more down the road. They do not enter our systems until their problems are already severe. Take a look at where they land on these continua in health, educational status, employment, and alcohol/drug use.

This chart, Governor, shows what happens when we intervene with this type of family. We can maintain through AFDC. We can remediate through education and job training or placement. We can prevent problems from getting worse through improving child health and development. You can see that while maintenance programs don't require an increase in effort or cost (unless the caseload expands), neither do they improve our situation over time.

Our agency data is limited, because it reflects people who are already in the system. We wanted to know more about people who are not yet in, so we met with parents and children in community forums organized by the United Way, and we met with nonprofit family service agencies and religious leaders in ten communities. We conclude that remediation improves family

outcomes but costs a lot to move families to an acceptable standard on the continuum. Prevention, particularly through an eclectic array of community-based services, is the most cost-effective approach over time because it produces tangible results, lessens the amount of remediation necessary and ultimately reduces caseloads over time.

This story is hypothetical. The assessment conducted by the policy team illustrates what can be done, not what is commonly done. The team was able to capture information about whole families and make comparisons between approaches based on knowledge of costs and results. They were able to distinguish between families with singular and multiple problems, they were able to see strengths as well as problems, and they were able to observe changes over time. Chapter Two suggests how such an assessment can be done.

**CHAPTER TWO:
ASSESSING THE
WELL-BEING OF
FAMILIES**

In Chapter One, we emphasized the importance of viewing the whole family over time. Each member brings multiple strengths and problems that affect the entire group, no matter how the family is configured. Problems and strengths become apparent well before family members enter the human service system, and they progress and change long after they leave.

In developing policy to enhance the well-being of families, it is important to understand how well families in the state are doing now. Properly constructed, an assessment will capture the complexities of families and the interrelationships of multiple events. It will reveal family strengths, not just weaknesses. It will help to distinguish symptoms from causes and build a better understanding of circumstances that influence family outcomes.

Knowing where you are is an important prerequisite to determining where you want to be and how to get there. An assessment provides a departure point for developing goals and strategies. It can be a catalyst for debating alternative futures. In their introduction to the Illinois *State of the Child* report, Testa and Lawlor wrote:

> *It is expected that different people will draw different*
> *conclusions, inferences, and solutions based on different values they*
> *associate with each indicator reported. It is our hope that the free*
> *exchange of beliefs and opinions, informed by fact, will both enlarge*

*and enrich the current debate about choices, priorities, and possible
directions for children's policy in Illinois.*[42]

Assessment begins with a few simple, logical questions, much like those
asked by the Governor in the preceding story: Who are our families? How well do
they function? Which ones are in trouble? How severely? Why? How well are
they served?

Asking these questions is easy. Answering them is not. While we have
lots of data about people and problems, we collect and organize the information
to reveal the condition of individuals, not families. We know about singular problems, not the interplay of multiple problems or strengths. We do not track families
over time, we take snapshots at crisis points.

In this chapter we propose a family-based approach. We begin by examining some of the questions that are the basis for developing a family assessment.
We suggest ways to obtain answers. Finally, we recommend ways to probe the
results and turn the data on their head, to be sure to get a full sense of conditions
and causes.

Ultimately, it may become necessary for states to redesign their systems
for gathering information. We recommend beginning with a more incremental
approach—start with what you have. No matter how simple or elaborate your
methodology may be, two factors lead all others in determining the utility of your
assessment. They are the relevance of the questions asked and how well the
inherent biases in the data are understood and accounted for. If you ask the right
questions and you know what the answers tell and don't tell you about the problem,
you are off to a good start.

Ask the Right Questions

The information we gather to tell us about ourselves responds to a variety
of questions. The census tells us how we grow and change every ten years. Crime
statistics tell us how safe our communities are. Birth and death records tell us
about our health and mortality. Educational testing tells us something about the
ability of the school-age population to read and reason. Data from human service
agencies reveal who is being served and at what cost.

While the information we gather is useful for its discrete purpose, it tells
us little about families. This is because our human service delivery system, for the

most part, is designed to work with individuals in response to specific problems, as we have discussed. Devising policies and systems in support of the entire family fell out of fashion after the settlement house movement in the early part of this century and has only recently returned as a plausible approach.

If families are the appropriate focus for policy, then policymakers must ask questions that lead analysts to find out about families:

Who are our families?

How might we describe the general population? How might we break the population into useful subsets to further enhance our understanding of who they are?

How well do our families function?

How well do our families provide security, sustenance, support, socialization, and stimulation?

What forces are influencing the ability of families to function well?

How are changes in the structure and routine of families affecting family functioning? How do local economic shifts, state budget cuts, tax policies, corporate policies, and insurance regulations affect family functioning?

Which families are in trouble?

What are the characteristics of families in trouble? Where are they? Are they concentrated geographically or are they dispersed? How do they compare with the general population?

What is the nature of their trouble and why?

What kinds of problems are they experiencing? How many families have multiple problems? What are the underlying causes?

What are their strengths?

Of the families you would expect to be in trouble, which are not and why? How many families with multiple problems actually improve their situations? What combination of internal strengths and external supports assists them in this process?

How well are they served?

Which families are getting services from state and local agencies? With what results? At what cost per family? Which families are getting services from nonprofit, and/or private service providers? With what results? At what cost per family? To what extent are families receiving services from more than one service provider or system? With what results? At what cost per family? How do families receiving services differ from families not receiving services?

How does the present compare with the past?

What are the possible explanations for these changes over time?

How does the present compare with the future?

What are the longer-term trends (state, national, and international) that are likely to affect families? What are the signals in the environment that suggest change? How are demographic, economic, and/or political shifts likely to influence families?

These questions are not carved in stone. They will, and should, vary from state to state. No matter what questions you pose, however, a few principles are important to consider. First, the questions should provide room to challenge assumptions about how you view families. For example, how to organize the population of families into meaningful subgroups is worth a hearty debate. If you choose to go with a structural cut—two parents versus a single parent—you are assuming that single-parent families are more likely to be in trouble. If you divide it according to income, you are making assumptions about the relative risk for families above and below the poverty line. Are there other ways to organize the information? What about families living in safe environments, or families able to meet daily nutritional requirements? Each cut has merit and limits. Be sure you know what they are, and then decide which is most appropriate for your analysis.

Second, the questions should push you to make useful comparisons. For example, a series of questions related to the services provided make the implicit assumption that services are better than no services. By asking a comparative question, looking at the population not receiving services, we push ourselves to recognize and challenge these assumptions. We also push ourselves to understand more about people and how they use services.

Comparisons are also useful over time. Often, in the policymaking process, we assume that current trends will continue. Often, we assume that the problems we face are unique to our generation. Often, we are wrong. But unless we systematically ask how things have developed over the years, and how they might change in the future, we are prone to be victims of the present.

Third, the questions should bring into focus both problems and strengths. It is just as valuable to know who is doing well under certain conditions as it is to know who is doing poorly. Since we hope that our policies ultimately will contribute to more people doing well, it is critical that we examine the nature of success.

Fourth, the questions should bring into view multiple problems and strengths. In his foreword to New York's *State of the Child* report, Joe Cocozza wrote:

> *We knew that the problems children and families experienced were complex and interrelated. In addition, we knew that to effectively address these difficulties we would need to examine them not in isolation from one another, but as a whole. Therefore, we began to seek a method to gather information and analyze trends involving the broadest possible range of issues.*[43]

Finally, the questions should explore the relationship of family well-being to other things. Everything from redistricting to budget cutbacks, from plant closings to growth management plans, can have a bearing on the options and choices for families. It is useful to identify those circumstances in the larger environment—the neighborhood, city, state, country, and world—that might be influencing families.

Get the Answers

Getting the answers is not easy, but it is possible. The approach we suggest below starts with what you have, and builds from there. Decide first what information would be adequate to satisfy your curiosity. Then determine what is already out there that fits the bill. Determine where there are gaps, and review a range of options for bridging them.

It is unlikely that you will develop an entirely new data system for assessing families immediately. Nor should you have to. Organizing and supplementing existing data collection efforts will go a long way toward getting the job done.

Determine What Information Will Provide Answers

Review your assessment questions and make a list of things you would like to know in order to satisfy your curiosity. For example, you want to assess the degree to which families in the state are able to feed, clothe, and ensure good health for themselves. What information, without regard to its current availability, would tell you something about how well families are providing sustenance? You might include things like nutritional status of children and families, food stamp participation, grocery store receipts, birth weight and prenatal care, income, Medicaid use, birth and death statistics.

Once you've made an exhaustive list, review it and refine it by asking: If we had this information, would it really tell us what we want to know about family functioning?

Colorado, for example, is developing a "Community Report Card." Each community will be asked to grade itself on whether it is good for families and children according to the following measures:[44]

COMMUNITY REPORT CARD—1991

☐NEIGHBORHOODS
  Are they safe and crime free?
☐SCHOOLS
  Are parents and businesses
  welcomed as partners?
☐TEENAGERS
  Are they able to find jobs?
☐PLAYGROUNDS
  Are they free from hazardous
  objects?
☐PARENTING
  Are parenting classes and
  support programs available?
☐SECURITY
  Are children free from abuse
  and neglect?
☐HEALTH INSURANCE
  Are families receiving adequate
  coverage?

☐PREGNANT WOMEN
  Are they receiving medical care
  and good nutrition?
☐YOUNG CHILDREN
  Are they all immunized against
  the seven major childhood
  diseases?
☐CHILD CARE
  Are all working parents able to
  receive quality, affordable child
  care?
☐ELECTED OFFICIALS
  Are children and families
  considered in planning for the
  future and in passing
  ordinances?

Find Out Who Is Gathering This Information

Much of what you want to know is already available. The New York *State Of The Child* report reflects data gathered from more than twenty federal, state, and municipal agencies. Many national data sets can be disaggregated to the state level. Those that cannot be disaggregated have the value of signaling national trends and issues that you may want to examine more closely within the state.

Existing data sources include the following:

- National Center on Health Statistics
- *Decennial Census* and *Current Population Survey*
- *Schools and Staffing Survey*
  (National Center on Education Statistics)
- AFDC Quality Control System
  (U.S. Department of Health and Human Services)
- *Survey of Income and Program Participation*
  (U.S. Department of Health and Human Services)
- Child Welfare Data
  (Voluntary Cooperative Information System, American Public Welfare Association)
- Reported Crime, Arrest Data, and Incarceration
  (Uniform Crime Report, U.S. Department of Justice)
- *National Longitudinal Survey*
  (U.S. Department of Labor, U.S. Census Bureau, and Ohio State University)
- *Panel Study on Income Dynamics*
  (University of Michigan and U.S. Department of Health and Human Services)
- *Kids Count Data Book: State Profiles of Child Well-Being* (The Annie Casey Foundation, Center for the Study of Social Policy)

While national data can inform your assessment, they are no substitute for your own information. Where national studies cannot be disaggregated to the state level, find some means to probe how closely your state mirrors national conditions.

Constructing a chart like the one below will help you sort out what is available, from whom, and how well it matches your needs.

SUSTENANCE

Examples of

Indicators	Source	(LEVEL:PERIOD:FOCUS)
Health		
Low Birth weight	National Center for Health Statistics (NCHS) Monthly Vital Statistics Report Also: State Department of Health Vital Statistics	(N,S,L:a,m:P,I)
Infant Mortality	NCHS Monthly Vital Statistics Report	(N,S,L:a,m:P,I)
Nutrition		
Food Stamp Participation	State welfare agency annual report	(S,L:a:F)
Grocery Consumption	Survey of grocery sales patterns for markets in poverty areas	(L:a:F)

Level—N = nat'l; S = state; L = local
Period—a = annual; q = quarterly; m = monthly; w = weekly
Focus—P = prenatal; I = infant; C = child; Y = youth; A = adult; E = elderly; F = family

Understand the Strengths and Limitations of Data

To avoid being misled by available data, it is important to recognize the purposes for which they are gathered, their limitations, and their inherent biases. Some of the limitations frequently encountered are discussed below:

Data Are Gathered For A Single Purpose.

Much of the readily available data are gathered by state agencies. Typically , the data are relevant only to the programs for which the agencies have responsibility or jurisdiction. As a result, these data reveal little about the totality of the problems, needs, and attributes of individuals, much less families.

Data Rarely Reflect Multiple Uses Of Services.

Data are gathered on specific services to clients—issuing food stamps, establishing eligibility for Medicaid or AFDC, providing nutrition, helping people find child care or enroll in job training. Many people use more than one service. But client records and agency reports treat cases, not people, failing to identify people using multiple services or having more than one problem.

Data Focus on Individuals, Not Families.

Because most of the data gathered concern individuals, it is difficult to assemble family data from existing records. It may be impossible to link the record for a single mother with social problems with the record for her child who is also in the system. Family issues, therefore, are overlooked.

Data Reflect Symptoms, Not Causes.

Demographic data—age, race, sex, marital status, education, and income level—are easy to obtain but are often viewed as surrogates for the underlying causes of problems that we do not measure directly. Divorce, for example, is one symptom of family dysfunction. The turmoil that can lead to divorce may, in some cases, pose greater risk than the act of divorce itself.[45] In other cases, the same turmoil may be present, but the culminating event may be something other than divorce.

Data Reflect Problems, Not Strengths.

Data are most often gathered to document a problem or to track those who have entered the human services system. For example, child abuse statistics are reported annually. Although most people treat their children well, there are no statistics on how well children are being treated.

Data Rarely Report Client Outcomes or Track What Happens Over Time.

Caseload data are not concerned with tracking people over time as they enter and exit programs. Agency data bases are typically set up to report how many clients are served and at what cost. At any time, agencies know who they are serving, but usually cannot distinguish among long- and short-term clients. Longitudinal studies that focus on outcomes are not widespread.

Anticipate Other Barriers To Getting Family-Focused Information

In addition to the inherent limitations of the data, a host of constraints rooted in law, standards, professional attitudes, and resource limitations pose challenges. These are difficult but not insurmountable. Here are five common problems:

- Agencies lack the money or expertise to gather data not mandated by their funders or required for the day-to-day conduct of business.
- Conflicts in professional standards, ideologies, and definitions may prevent agreement on what data to collect—adult literacy professionals may disagree with secondary school administrators on what constitutes illiteracy, for example.
- Legal guarantees of privacy, such as the protection of medical records or the sealing of juvenile court records limit access to information.
- Agencies may suspect that others will use their data against them—to cut budgets, to set up competing programs, or to criticize their performance.
- Agencies may view data gathering as diverting time or resources from serving clients.

Fill in the Gaps

Pulling together existing sources of information will provide important information about families, but it will also highlight gaps. You may discover, for example, that the data reveal the numbers of children living apart from their fathers, but do not say much about the bonds formed between fathers and their children regardless of where they live. In addition, there is little available in existing data sets to help us understand peer relationships, future aspirations, or expectations.

There are a number of ways to enrich your knowledge of families at a relatively low cost. You can ask the graduate school of public policy at your state university to work with you in gathering information. Faculty and graduate students could conduct surveys of high-risk families. You can join forces with family-focused organizations such as Family Service America or your statewide United Way. These organizations gather information on community-based services and provide quick access to service providers. They may also be willing to help set up focus groups with service providers and participants.

Public opinion polls are also a rich resource. Many statewide or regional public opinion research institutes are willing to share their data. In addition, two major national archives, the Roper Center for Public Opinion Research and the Louis Harris Data Center are storehouses of data collected by several national polling organizations.

You also can go out and conduct your own interviews of community leaders, church groups, and family members in selected communities. Add a few questions to existing intake forms or regularly conducted surveys to get more family-focused data. Talk to pollsters in the state about inserting questions about family aspirations and expectations into an existing poll. Here are a few specific approaches to consider:

Quality Assurance.
Some agencies (welfare departments in particular) are required to survey clients to determine rates of fraud and abuse. In addition to asking clients questions for administrative accountability, analysts can insert questions that focus on outcomes for the individual and family members. Because the survey is mandated, the cost of adding such questions is greatly reduced.

Survey Research.
A survey of households to collect data on each family member is probably the best way to fill in the gaps. The most efficient way to complete such a survey is to employ the methodology of the U.S. Bureau of Census. The Texas Department of Human Services, for example, periodically conducts a special statewide census to assess needs for human services. Their data can easily be used to understand status and outcomes.

Existing Needs Assessments.
Many public and private agencies assess community needs for their services. These assessments are often required by state and federal laws or regulations. They are hardly used by policymakers. Program managers use them for internal reporting if at all. Analysts should find out what assessments have been made and extract data for their needs. Local agencies could restructure their data

collection to help this task. Local agencies can share the costs of data collection among themselves.

Focus Groups.

Even after completing these types of studies, questions will remain about linkages across family members. These questions can be answered through focus groups. A small group—ten to fifteen single mothers on welfare or participating in JTPA, for example—can be questioned about their problems and use of different programs. This is also a good means for identifying strengths. A group of Iowa lawmakers, conducting a focus group with teen mothers on welfare, discovered a great deal about the energy and effort these women put forth despite significant obstacles.

National Data.

The federal government has created useful national data bases, which include the Decennial Census, Current Polpulation Survey, Survey of Income and Program Participation, and the Uniform Crime Statistics. Other national surveys, like the *Panel Study of Income Dynamics* and *Kids Count*, published by the Center for the Study of Social Policy, are also available. Although many of these are not state-specific, national data can be used to suggest possible state issues where local data do not exist. The data can be used to help determine where to target your information-gathering efforts.

Probe for Causes

Your assessment should attempt to explain, not simply describe, the condition of families. Explaining involves offering several plausible reasons for behavior, then probing for the most likely. This approach requires pushing beyond the surface of the facts. Consider our hypothetical state. The largest city in the state has a school dropout rate of 35 percent. The range of possible explanations for poor school performance could include a recent influx of first-generation American children into the school system, a precipitous rise in profits in the underground narcotics industry, the absence of an ethnocentric curriculum, the average grade attainment of the parents of school-age children in the district, or the manner in which enrollment data are maintained.

If 35 percent of the students entering school drop out by the age of sixteen, 65 percent do not. What causes these students to stay in? They live in the same neighborhood and have a similar demographic profile. What is different for these kids? Are they using services more effectively? Are their parents high school graduates? Were they better prepared for school? Are there significant differences among schools in the district?

It is important to explore underlying causes for both failure and success. In Chapter One, we discussed risk factors such as a high concentration of poverty, poor educational attainment of parents, prevalence of crime and drugs in a community, large percentages of teen parents and single-parent households—all associated with poor family functioning. But if we stop our probing at this point, we miss something important. Many families do well despite the presence of such risk factors. They may have better coping skills, more information about services, or better connections to the job market. Digging beneath the surface to determine possible explanations for both success and failure is important, because it gives you better leads on strategies.

Stay on Track

There is no shortage of information. Your data analysts and department heads will be quick to provide you with stacks of charts, tables, and reports. The information will be impressive. It may also be of little use. Often data packaging has such allure that we unwittingly accept it. We substitute what the packagers want to provide for what we need. Don't be tempted.

No matter how many sophisticated models or multicolored graphics you are presented with, be sure that they are on track. Be in control of the questions and demand that the answers be about:

- *Families,* not just individuals
- *Progress over time,* not just at crisis points
- *Outcomes,* not just inputs
- *Strengths,* not just problems
- *Multiple strengths and problems,* not just singular events

While a comprehensive assessment of family well-being may not be immediately achievable, it is a worthwhile aim for several reasons. First, because the human service delivery system (and data collection) is so fragmented, decision makers cannot know, for example, if a small group of people consume many expensive services or if a large group of people consume a few services. By stabilizing and improving the family situation of a few intensive users, the government can serve more people effectively.

Second, by understanding better how outcomes tend to cluster in families, remediation programs can be provided to improve the key outcomes associated with overall family progress.

Third, you can begin to determine where prevention programs can be applied most cost effectively. For example, schools and human service agencies today offer prevention programs to nearly everyone because we cannot identify who really needs them. Measles are devastating to a few children, but not to most people. Because we do not know who will be harmed, we must immunize everyone. Conducting a family-based assessment helps to better determine which groups will benefit most from prevention.

Fourth, a good assessment is the foundation for more effective program evaluation and policy accountability systems, as discussed in Chapter Five.

Unfortunately, inadequate assessment and documentation of family well-being is not the only challenge confronting policymakers who wish to improve results for families. Setting outcome-oriented, family-focused goals is the next challenge we will examine.

HAPPY ENDINGS

We cannot know what will happen to Rose and Michael. But as policymakers we can envision what we would like to happen. Here is one version of two happy endings.

A Family Plan:
Better Outcomes for Rose's Family

A "happy ending" for Rose's family could look something like this: Maria, Rose's mother, has a plan for the future. She has written down the plan with the help of a woman friend (a person trained to help families like Rose's) who has been visiting the home regularly. The plan accounts for each member of Rose's family living at home. Maria attends a parent support group in her community one night a week. In the group, she talks about what she wants to do for each member of her family, including herself and her own mother.

The fights between her and Rose's sister have diminished. She doesn't let her older daughter take food and other supplies from the house, but she has gone with her to the local food pantry to help her get food for the children. She plans to go with her daughter to take the children for a health screening and get information on family planning.

One afternoon a week, Rose's mother sits down and reviews Rose's school work with her. She received help from Rose's teacher in figuring out what to concentrate on. The same friend who helped her write the plan and took her to the parent support group set up the meeting with Rose's teacher. During the meeting, Maria was able to talk a little with the teacher about what it is like at home—about the uncle and the grandmother. The teacher suggested that Rose and her mother write a story together about Rose's grandmother and how she is gradually getting well.

This meeting turned out to be beneficial for Rose's mother as well. She realized that she needed some help with her own reading and writing skills. As soon as the grandmother, who is recuperating at home, is able to get her own meals and move around the apartment, Rose's mother will start a literacy class in the mornings. For the first time, Rose hears her mother talk about looking for an office job.

Rose's grandmother is rapidly improving. A nurse checks in on her once a week at home, making sure that she is taking her medication, eating right and exercising enough. She arrives in the afternoon right after Rose and her younger sister come home from school. She always visits awhile with them. Sometimes Rose's mother goes out for a soda with a friend while the nurse is there. Last week, the nurse talked with Rose about the health clinic in the neighborhood. The nurse is planning to take Rose, her younger sister, and two school friends there next month for a health screening. But before talking with the girls, the nurse talked it over with Rose's mother. Together, they set the date, and Maria wrote it into her family plan.

One problem has been difficult for Rose's family—her younger brother. He still prefers to hang out, take drugs, and not go to school. After many agonizing hours in the support group, Rose's mother tells her thirteen-year-old son that he must either go into a drug treatment program or leave home. She makes it clear that she means it! It is easier to do, knowing that there is an available slot in a nearby program.

Rose is happiest about her father. He spends more time in the apartment now—sometimes he is there three or four nights a week. He used to drop by only to give Rose's mother some money, and after a while, they would fight (usually about his drinking) and he would go off to his cousin's house, often for weeks at a time. Rose's mother has put him in the family plan, too. She hopes he will enroll in job training and cut down on his drinking. She spends a lot of time talking about this situation in the parent support group, now that things are more settled with the children.

The friend who helped Rose's mother with the plan continues to keep in touch. She phones the house twice a week, and she always stops by if she can't get in touch with Maria. Her contact helped to avoid a family crisis last month when the landlord threatened eviction due to nonpayment of rent. She was able to help Rose's mother figure out how to handle the situation, and the landlord agreed to wait two extra weeks for payment.

No Longer Alone: A Future for Michael

Should Michael be considered a family? He has already left home. Any chance for prevention or early intervention with Michael and his birth or adoptive families is long gone. Michael has violated the safety of others. Furthermore, the state has already invested funds and energy in

Michael with little apparent return. Perhaps it is time to give up on him. But a happy ending can be imagined for Michael also.

Michael ended up in the state conservation corps. He spends his days in a closely supervised, well-structured work program and in the classroom. Despite the fact that he graduated from high school, his reading, writing, and math skills were at an eighth-grade level. His course work, taught and supervised by the local community college, is a combination of applied basic skills development, career exploration, and life skills development. How did this happen?

Even though Michael, an independent adult, was tried and found guilty, an innovative prison alternative program was available for him as a first-time offender. The program started out with four months of residential treatment. Toward the end of the program, Michael developed a plan to bring in several members of his adoptive family and friends, with the help of his counselor and parole officer. This group, along with several of Michael's new friends from the treatment program, met once a week during the last month of his stay in the program. They all agreed to work with Michael as a support group when he left the program and went into the conservation corps. Together, they talked about a good place for Michael to be stationed, what support he would need, and how he would obtain it. During those group meetings, Michael was able to tell his adoptive father some important things. He made amends for past mistakes and was forgiven.

Michael has good days and bad. Sometimes he longs for the magic of his days as a basketball star. But when he is low or fed up with having to work so hard, he can call his father or a few friends. The community service he does helps him to feel better about himself. He sees his skills growing and feels that he just might have a future. He knows that he is yet not ready, but he imagines that some day, with support, he will be able to make restitution to the store clerk he nearly killed.

CHAPTER THREE:
POLICY GOALS
AND OBJECTIVES

Why Set Direction?

A vision, like those you just read, paints a picture of what you hope the future will be. It is more than a two-sentence mission statement. It can be a creative and energizing step in the otherwise analytical process of policy development. Creating a vision helps you to decide where you want to go with your family policy. It is a step that logically precedes the development of policy goals and objectives.

Policymakers should take the time to envision a future for families. The benefits are many. First, the vision becomes the point of comparison for the assessment work described in Chapter Two. Second, when expressed to the public, the vision taps into people's broad hopes and expectations, galvanizing their support for the journey.

Third, the process of creating the vision exposes differences among policymakers early in the policy development, when they can be explored and resolved. Negative reactions to language and jargon, once uncovered, can be easily corrected. For example, one family policy development team discovered that "placement" is considered a positive outcome in the job training world, but a negative outcome in the child welfare world. Fourth, when jointly developed by public and private sector policymakers from different constituencies, backgrounds, and perspectives, the vision becomes the fertile ground for common commitment to policy goals and objectives.

Of course the most important reason for having a vision, and the policy goals and objectives that flow from it, is to set a clear direction for your family policy. Operating without it is like crossing Boston in rush hour—if you do not have a good road map with a circled destination, sign posts, and easy-to-understand directions, you can make a wrong turn and end up five miles from nowhere.

The Three Components of Direction

The next two chapters explore three components of this road map: policy goals and objectives, strategies, and implementation planning. Think of these components as destinations, paths, and directions.

The destination.
There are two types of destinations. A policy goal is a broad statement of the ultimate purpose of the policy. Its accomplishment usually stretches well into the future. It may be like the end of the rainbow—always clear, but forever just out of reach. Policy objectives are specific, achievable, outcome-oriented descriptions of desired policy results. These destinations are checkpoints on the journey to the rainbow's end. They can be early in the journey (first year) or late (five to ten years). Policy objectives are subject to adjustment, while policy goals most often remain the same. Outcome-oriented objectives state desired results for people (Rose, Michael, and their families) or for systems (state and local agencies and their programs).

The paths.
Strategies—a set of activities or programs combined in a particular way—are alternative paths to the destination. A program is a well-defined set of activities directed at a particular problem and/or target population with dedicated funding streams. A program can be a strategy, but strategies usually involve more than one program. Strategies change over time, adjusting to political, social, and fiscal conditions. There is always more than one path to any destination. Strategic options must be available, though one path may be the best for a variety of reasons.

The directions.
Implementation plans are detailed directions on how to move down the path. They specify the mode of travel, the drivers, signposts, rules of the road,

and estimated times of departure and arrival. The clearer the directions, the less opportunity for wrong turns. At the same time, however, the drivers must be prepared to respond if road conditions change.

Families and individuals who need help, service providers, program administrators, and policymakers all need a clear road map, though the map looks different to each group. The "happy endings" described at the beginning of this chapter for Rose and her family and for Michael are not just a fantasy. These destinations can become real for individuals and families across the United States. They can become real if Governors and other policymakers have a conceptual framework about families, if they assess the extent and severity of the problems that confront them, understand probable causes, and envision measurable outcomes for new policy development. This chapter offers several steps in setting outcome-oriented policy goals and objectives for families.

Envision Results for Families and Individuals

Results for individuals and their families are changes in risk status or functioning. Whatever dimension is used, outcomes should be conceptualized on a continuum to describe progress over time from a baseline toward an expected future. Review the changes in Rose's family and Michael's situation. These families are still very much at risk, but definite progress has been made. Let's look at the outcomes by family function.

Providing Sustenance.

The entire health status for Rose's family is improving. Her nieces go to the clinic for screening and treatment, perhaps through the Early and Periodic Screening, Diagnosis and Treatment program (EPSDT), a Medicaid-funded program. Rose's grandmother is recovering and soon will be able to function independently. Rose and her sister also are screened for health problems and referred for treatment. Counting Rose's older sister, six members of Rose's family will receive information on pregnancy prevention. Nutrition has improved for Rose's entire family, including the older sister and children.

While obtaining or bettering employment is a goal for Rose's sister, brother, and father, other problems such as alcohol and drug abuse have to be resolved first. Michael, however, can point with pride to improved outcomes, such as job readiness, job skills, and actual full-time employment.

Providing Support.

Rose's mother is better able to give and seek support. The key indicators of improved family functioning are reduced conflict in the home (between Rose's mother and older sister and between her mother and father), the ability of Rose's mother to cope with existing problems (such as the father's drinking and the brother's drug abuse), and improved problem solving (avoiding the eviction crisis, for example). For Michael, even though he is not living with his family, he has reconnected with a support group. His own self-esteem and interpersonal skills have improved.

Providing Stimulation.

Rose's school performance is improving, as is her sister's. Rose is receiving more support from her mother, as well as from her teacher, who now knows more about Rose. Rose's mother will improve her own education status through literacy classes. Michael has strengthened his basic skills.

Envision Changes for Systems

Michael, Rose, and their families had to change some old patterns to accomplish the results described above, as did the systems that served them. These changes can also be described as outcomes.

Family-oriented services that are responsive and flexible.

Rose's mother received help initially from a single point of contact, a woman who related to her as a knowledgeable friend, not as a professional case manager. This woman visited the home, frequently at first. Her approach was to help Rose's mother take responsibility for family members. She did not "take charge" unless it was absolutely necessary, but she worked a lot behind the scenes. Based on the mother's plan, she organized a meeting between Rose's mother and her teacher. She introduced Maria to the parent support group, gave her information about the community food pantry and the health clinic, and encouraged her to take her older daughter there. As the family situation improved, the helper's visits gradually became less frequent, but regular contact did not stop. This arrangement enabled immediate response when a crisis occurred.

Community-based, integrated services.

Rose's family case manager coordinated with a number of other community services. Another professional, the community nurse, came to the home and interacted with the family. Clearly, she had communicated with the case manager, as she timed her arrival to give Rose's mother a break from the family, supported the mother's responsibility for family decisions, and worked within the framework of the mother's family plan. The case manager also referred Rose's mother to other community services, such as the food pantry and the clinic. With the mother's permission, the case manager has shared key information with community service providers: the center offering the parent support class, the health clinic, the visiting nurse, the school, and the drug treatment center.

Coordinated state services.

Successful support for Michael resulted from collaboration among several state systems and programs: the court system, the correctional system (including institutional, parole and community services divisions), the state education and community college systems, the employment and training system, the mental health system, and the state conservation corps.

Note that many activities were undertaken on behalf of Rose and her family and Michael of which they were unaware. These included assessment, documentation, planning, communication, data gathering and analysis, and evaluation. Although families must be involved in any decision making that directly affects them, they do not need to see these activities. We do not need to see where and how telephone wires, sewer systems, and electric cables connect in order to walk, ride, and conduct business in the city. The road map of these inner workings should be of no concern to us, as long as we can make decisions and accomplish our goals. The same is true for Rose, Michael, and their families.

Develop Family Outcome Statements

A Governor's State of the State or Budget Address offer the opportunity to transform a vision into something more specific. After her election, the Governor in Chapter Two reviewed her campaign promises. She knew that the press, the legislature, and various constituencies would be reviewing them as well. The advocacy community assumed that safe meant free from street and domestic violence, abuse, and neglect and that secure meant free from hunger and inadequate housing and accessible to nutrition and health services. The education community assumed that quality education meant reduced class sizes and higher pay for teachers and aides. The business community assumed that quality education meant a higher percentage of high school graduates with solid basic skills and improved technological training. That's the beauty of policy goals—they mean many things to many different constituencies.

In an environment of limited resources, however, the Governor must build agreement within her state around a few key outcomes. To be successful she must gain support for specifics. Why outcomes, not programs? First, policy outcomes clarify the purpose of the policy to those whose support is needed and those who are responsible for implementation. Second, those who have a stake in the policy may be willing to support the desired results, even though they may differ on strategies, programs, or required funding. Agreement on outcomes increases the likelihood of successful negotiation in these other areas. Third, outcomes form the basis of a policy accountability system that Governors can use to hold agency heads accountable. Finally, specifying desired results increases political credibility, especially if accomplishments can be measured against expectations and those expectations are adjusted and renewed over time. Here are some family outcomes the Governor might consider. Note that they are arrayed by key family function, not by typical state agency.

Providing Security

- Child and spouse abuse will decline
- The number of first-time juvenile offenders will decline
- Juvenile recidivism will decline
- The number of probationers and parolees violating substance abuse special conditions will decline
- Families will live in decent and affordable housing
- Fewer children and adolescents will abuse drugs or alcohol

Providing Sustenance

- Heads of families on welfare will get jobs at liveable wages or, at a minimum, increase their earnings
- Jobs in the state will pay "family wages"

- Noncustodial parents will pay child support
- Fewer of the state's babies will be born with low birth weight
- All two-year-olds will have received appropriate immunizations
- All families will have increased access to basic health services.

Providing Support

- Child abuse and neglect will decline
- Gang violence will decline
- The number of children entering out-of-home foster care will go down
- The number of teen pregnancies will decline.
- The number of children in out-of-state placements—will decline
- Fewer children and adolescents will abuse drugs or alcohol

Providing Socialization

- Students will start first grade ready to learn
- More noncustodial parents will maintain positive contact with their children
- The birth rate among young teens will be reduced
- Fewer children and adolescents will abuse drugs or alcohol

Providing Stimulation

- The numbers of parents involved in educational planning for their children will increase
- Students will achieve a high school diploma and will be prepared for post-secondary education, employment, or both
- The skills of the state's workforce will be upgraded
- Youth will be functionally literate in reading, writing, computation and citizenship

Policymakers may also want to specify several system outcomes. Washington State has developed criteria for the system it thinks will serve families best.

Their system will:

- Offer services that are culturally relevant
- Ensure services are locally designed and oriented
- Provide access to a wide variety of services regardless of point of entry
- Coordinate services provided to the family
- Provide funding mechanisms that are flexible enough to be responsive to family needs
- Provide incentives for local participation and partnerships with local agencies and businesses
- Allow assessment of the programs made by families toward their maximum level of self-sufficiency
- Establish lead responsibility for adhering to a plan of action and service delivery developed and agreed to by the family and service agencies
- Build capacity in the community for addressing family needs

Develop Indicators for Key Outcomes

The outcome statements above are policy goals; they give a destination, but not the signposts for determining progress. To develop signposts, policymakers must determine indicators. Chapter Two talked about the importance of developing indicators for the family outcomes listed above. Indicators of accomplishment of systems' goals are often easier to obtain. Changes in existing program reports, supplemented by periodic consumer and provider surveys, should indicate progress toward most outcomes.

Set Targets for Accomplishment: Measurable, Outcome-Oriented Objectives

After careful data review, policymakers may wish to set targets for achievement of key outcomes. Policymakers can visualize these targets as moveable points along an outcome continuum for specific target groups of families or individuals. Certainly, there are risks in setting targets. Desired results may not be achieved. The media may use specific objectives to pummel decision makers for lack of initiative, follow-through or resources. If targets are adjusted, decision makers may be open to the charge of inconsistency. These risks are outweighed by the benefits of having a well-functioning accountability system, and they can be overcome with timely information flow and a clear political communications strategy. Chapters Five and Six will explore these points more fully.

Select Policy Objectives

Plausibility and feasibility are the key criteria for selecting policy objectives. Plausibility answers the question, "What evidence exists to show that pursuing this objective will lead to the desired outcome?" Feasibility answers the question, "Are all the necessary resources available to accomplish the objective?"

Four methods are used for determining plausibility: research or evaluation data, logic or common sense, expert opinion, and consensus. An objective supported by research may be the best approach, but in the government, data-based information is often unavailable. Many policymakers must rely on a creative combination of all methods. Determining feasibility requires estimating the costs of a wide range of implementation strategies, as well as reviewing time and personnel requirements. It is also important to estimate the amount of leadership, attention, and political capital the Governor and other top-level policymakers must expend to accomplish the objective.

Let's assume that the Governor in Chapter Two has conducted an assessment of family status in her state, as well as a careful scan of her existing services, programs, budget, and political environment. After considerable analysis, senior policy staff and the agency subcabinet recommend six priority objectives to strengthen and support families in her state. They are:

1. By 1995, increase by 30 percent the numbers of families getting off welfare due to an increase in earnings.

2. By 1995, decrease the number of low birth-weight babies to fewer than 5 per 100.

3. By 1998, reduce first-time juvenile offenders by 50 percent in five specific geographic areas that have high juvenile crime rates and high family density.

4. By 1998, reduce by 75 percent the number of children placed out-of-home or in institutions because of mental health problems.

5. By the year 2000, 90 percent of children in the state will start first grade ready to learn.

6. By the year 2000, 90 percent of the state's students will achieve a high school diploma and will be prepared for post-secondary education, employment, or both.

Chapter Three opened with a description of two potential happy endings. Let's check the logic of this Governor's policy as it has developed so far. Will accomplishing these objectives help Rose and Michael and their families? State and local efforts to achieve the first objective will assist Rose's sister and her family. Strategies related to objectives two, three, and four will offer services to Rose, her friends, and her brother. Objective five relates directly to Rose's nieces. Michael is the direct beneficiary of objective six. Many other objectives might have been chosen to improve family functioning in general, and Rose's and Michael's family situations in particular. If these six, chosen because of a state's unique circumstances, are accomplished, many families will benefit.

**CHAPTER FOUR:
STRATEGIES FOR
SUCCESS**

Successful Strategies

A successful strategy is any path that gets you to your destination. Some paths are better than others; they may be more efficient, more challenging or dramatic, or less risky. There are many criteria by which to choose strategies. Unfortunately for the policymaker, choosing is not the major difficulty. The difficulty is having something from which to choose. Too often, policymakers approach the task of strategy design with a sense of desperation, like a drowning man grabbing any stick that floats by.

This chapter offers an approach designed to build options. The chapter presents five steps for building and selecting successful strategies. First, review outcomes, targets, and probable causes. Second, imagine all the possible paths that might lead to desired results. Third, place existing, redirected, and new activities and programs along these paths. Fourth, think beyond old roles and responsibilities. Finally, select on the basis of key criteria and begin to plan.

Review Outcomes, Targets, and Probable Causes

Start your strategy development by reviewing the outcomes you hope to achieve. Assume, for example, that you want to strengthen the ability of families to provide sustenance. A specific outcome, as a result of your efforts is healthier babies. You have established a target of fewer than 5 per 100 low birth-weight babies.

Next, consider the proximal causes of low birth-weight babies. They include: poor prenatal care; smoking; inadequate nutrition exercise and sleep; and alcohol and drug abuse. But what causes poor prenatal care? What causes a pregnant women to smoke, eat and sleep poorly, or abuse alcohol or drugs? These questions are more difficult to answer with certainty. A review of the literature, discussion with experts, and analysis of state and national data, reveal the primary cause of poor prenatal care to be lack of access to health care services, particularly for poor women in disadvantaged communities and young unmarried women.[46] A convergence of individual, family, and community factors promote and reinforce a woman's decision to smoke, take drugs, or care for herself and her baby. Self-esteem, peer pressure, role models, family patterns, availability of alcohol and drugs, health information, and community values all contribute to the decision to abuse alcohol and drugs.[47]

Imagine Possible Paths

Start with where you would like to be. Imagine that you have achieved your desired results. Now consider all the possible paths that you could have taken to get to there.

There are at least three strategic paths to healthy babies: good pre-natal care, promotion of healthy lifestyle choices, and the prevention of unplanned pregnancies. Let's apply our analysis to the case of Rose's family. Rose's sister has a healthy baby. How did this happen? First, prenatal care was available and affordable. Second, Rose's sister decided to use it. She understood the benefits of care; she knew that it was available and that she could get to it easily using public transportation. She had heard that the workers at the clinic were friendly and easy to talk to. Finally, she received something each time she attended the clinic—a coupon book for goods and services that she wanted.

A second path is promotion of healthy lifestyle choices on the part of the pregnant women. Rose's sister was determined to have a healthy baby. She signed up for the Women, Infants, and Children (WIC) supplementary nutrition program. She stopped smoking and did not take a drink during her pregnancy. She stayed away from her friends who took drugs. Why? Messages in her family and in the community reinforced the fact that such behaviors would lead to a healthier baby. Her welfare caseworker, who signed her up for WIC, gave her additional information and encouraged her to enroll in a family support group held twice weekly in her community—with child care provided. If Rose's sister had been addicted to drugs or alcohol, immediate referral—and entrance into—a treatment program would have been an obvious first step.

A third strategic path to healthy babies is the prevention of unplanned pregnancies. Rose is clearly at risk of an unplanned pregnancy but does not get pregnant. Why? She has access to good information, basic health services, and contraceptive devices. Furthermore, her mother and older sister have taken the time to explain to Rose what parenting is really like. Finally, a special program at her school is involving her in interesting activities after school and on weekends. She is feeling good about herself and having fun.

Looking back from a future that includes healthy babies, the strategic thinker is struck by several common themes. All the paths that reduce the occurrence of low birth-weight infants appear to be interrelated. They all require good information, available and accessible services, individual knowledge and positive choice, and family and community influence. Each separate path, whether pregnancy prevention, healthy life choices, or access to health care converges at the community level. But what is most striking is that this road map (see Figure 3) does not resemble at all the current configuration of strategies, services, and programs (see Figure 4). One, the current categorical system, is a confusing maze of separate programs, eligibility requirements, and geographical service areas. The other is a network of interconnecting roads with clear road signs right in the community. Unfortunately, most families and children who need help have to walk forward into the maze. Clearly, attaching new programs to the categorical maze will not make it any easier to traverse. To effectively help families and children, the policymaker must take another step in the strategic thinking process.

Position Programs Strategically: Two Approaches to Systems Change

How can we reconfigure categorical services into effective strategic paths? Four steps are involved. First, review and sort all existing programs, eliminating or reducing those that are ineffective or not part of the strategic path. Second, retool existing programs so that they lead to better results and reinforce each other. Third, fill service gaps or invent new approaches where needed. Fortunately, several states have taken the lead and offer some lessons. This section

Figure 3

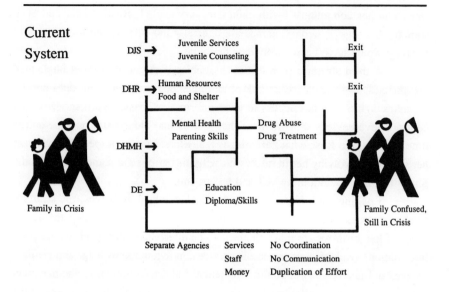

Current System

DJS → Juvenile Services / Juvenile Counseling — Exit

DHR → Human Resources / Food and Shelter — Exit

DHMH → Mental Health / Parenting Skills — Drug Abuse / Drug Treatment

DE → Education / Diploma/Skills

Family in Crisis

Family Confused, Still in Crisis

Separate Agencies   Services   No Coordination
                      Staff   No Communication
                      Money   Duplication of Effort

Figure 4

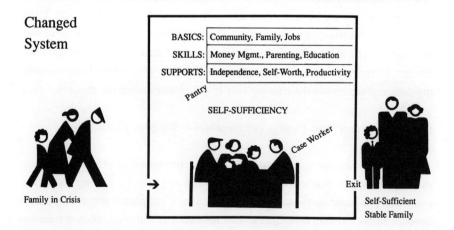

Changed System

BASICS:	Community, Family, Jobs
SKILLS:	Money Mgmt., Parenting, Education
SUPPORTS:	Independence, Self-Worth, Productivity

Pantry

SELF-SUFFICIENCY

Case Worker

Family in Crisis

Exit

Self-Sufficient Stable Family

*Figure adapted from the Maryland Academy team.

explores how two states have moved to reform their systems on behalf of families and children. To better understand these examples, we must review the steps each state took in developing its family policy.

Maryland

In May 1989, Governor Schaefer appointed a Special Secretary for Children, Youth, and Families and charged her with forming an interagency subcabinet focusing on family preservation. He further requested that this subcabinet work closely with his Employment and Training Council, which is accountable for coordinated work force investment policies. Together, these two groups, the core of which made up Maryland's family policy team, were to address the total needs of families and children.

Determine outcomes.

The team began by defining "family" and envisioning what healthy families looked like. A family was defined as "one or more adults who join together to provide care, support, and nurturance for a child, children, or each other regardless of where they live." The team decided to focus on those families whose quality of life is affected by poverty, education deficits, health problems, and family instability.

An impressive array of outcomes were chosen by the team as goals for increasing the number of safe, stable, nurturing, self-sufficient families. For example, Maryland has planned that by the year 2000, 95 percent of its students will start first grade ready to learn, and that 100 percent of its graduates will be functionally literate in reading, writing, mathematics, and citizenship. The state committed to increase the number of at-risk families participating in self-sufficiency programs and to ensure that these programs achieved results: a placement rate after job training of 85 percent and a wage at placement at 110 percent of the lower living index.

Family health and well-being were also important to the Governor and his team. The team planned to reduce by 75 percent the number of children placed out-of-home or in institutions because of mental health problems. They wanted all jurisdictions to have infant mortality rates far lower than the surgeon general's figures. Another objective was to reduce by 70 percent the drug or alcohol abuse in children and adolescents, as measured by the statewide student survey. The team planned to reduce child abuse and neglect by 25 percent each, decrease by

10 percent the number of repeat calls of spouse abuse, and reduce by 50 percent the number of children entering out-of-home care.

Imagine possible strategic paths.

The Maryland team recognized that to achieve these objectives the state would need more than existing agency programs or add-ons to the categorical system. They were committed to radically restructuring their investment in families. Their guiding principles for new strategies stipulated that they be (a) *integrated* in both planning and service delivery; (b) *flexible* in use of fiscal and human resources and in community design; (c) *accessible*—understood, convenient, affordable, and appropriate; (d) *accountable* for outcomes and fiscal management; and (e) *grounded* in partnership at the state and local level.

Furthermore, Maryland determined that state and local delivery systems should: assess family strengths as well as needs, develop a comprehensive plan of family services, provide joint intake or a single point of access for service, use an integrated case management model, give families priority access to developmentally appropriate core agency services, work in a partnership relationship with the family who needs help, and be held accountable across agencies for results.

Position existing, redirected, and new programs strategically.

First, Maryland reviewed their existing programs. In addition to operating welfare reform, the Job Training Partnership Act (JTPA); Medicaid; and other traditional, categorical education and health programs, the state is piloting child welfare system reform and several types of integrated, community-based, family programs.

Several counties are operating a child welfare reform project, funded in part by the Annie E. Casey Foundation, which focuses on an interagency planning process and an integrated case management system that links all providers. The purpose of this family preservation program is to prevent out-of-home placement and return children currently in out-of-home placements to a well-functioning family environment.

Maryland also has sixteen family-oriented, community-based programs that attempt to integrate some services. Thirteen of these programs, operated by the Maryland Department of Human Resources (DHR) historically have focused on family support, including such services as outreach, family assessment, case management or service brokering, and child development and parent education.

Two, run by the Governor's Employment and Training Council (GETC), historically have focused on job readiness, training, and education. One program is
operated by Baltimore city in a housing project.

After completing a review of the policy objectives, strategic paths, and
existing programs, the state felt that innovation was needed in four areas. First,
ongoing state-level coordination of policy and programs for families and children
had to be assured. Second, the state had to both empower and provide incentives
for broad-scale, local integrated planning and services implementation. Third, a
model or models of local integrated services had to be developed for possible
statewide replication. Fourth, a system of accountability had to be designed for
the new integrated approaches.

State-level policy/program coordination.

The Maryland legislature reorganized and strengthened The Office for Children,
Youth, and Families. This office was established as a part of the Executive Department on July 1, 1990, and is charged with (a) examining public and private programs
to identify duplications, inefficiencies, and unmet needs; (b) consulting with the
secretaries of the Departments of Health and Mental Health, Human Resources,
Juvenile Services, and Education, to develop an interagency plan that reflects the
priorities for children and an interagency budget that identifies and collates all
state expenditures for children; and (c) providing technical assistance to local
jurisdictions in planning and implementing interagency service delivery systems
for children, youth, and families.

Empowerment/incentives for local integrated services.

In 1990, the Maryland legislature passed legislation authorizing key
reforms in services delivery to children in foster care and families. These reforms
are being expanded gradually to all counties. Key components include:

- A contract signed by the state with the local jurisdiction (county) to
  implement systems reform along the lines envisioned by the family
  policy team. The contract defines a target population, core services,
  and a local governance structure. While no new funds are available,
  the state can offer the county a pool of flexible funds, collected from
  other programs, upon which the county can draw. The state works

closely with the county, providing technical assistance and generic case-management training.

- A $7.3 million pot of flexible funds (gathered from a line-by-line budget analysis—conducted jointly by the Governor's office and legislative staff—of the budgets of the Maryland Departments of Human Resources, Health and Mental Hygiene, Juvenile Services, and Education) to serve a specific target population of children and their families.

- An incentive to counties that enables them to keep a portion of the dollars they save by redirecting services away from out-of-state placement to in-state placement and away from foster care to family preservation.

Multiple models for local integrated services.
The Office for Children, Youth, and Families initially thought that one state model could appropriately integrate the two existing family initiatives—the family investment centers operated by GETC, and the family support centers operated by DHR. Although both models have several common components—outreach; case management; and access or referral to health, child care, literacy, parent education, and other services—each has a unique tone and focus. The family support centers stress family development, building trust, and internal motivation over time. GETC centers stress an external objective— family self-sufficiency (i.e., employment)- and the activities that will move the parent toward that objective.

Motivated by a desire for simplicity and clarity, the collaborative policy development team struggled to develop a "neat package" that contained all elements. But the pressure to decide on one model had the opposite effect. Underlying differences of perspective and approach surfaced. Polarization intensified. Eventually, the team concluded that diversity was not only necessary, but desirable. In fact, different models could strengthen each other. Each attracts and holds different types of families. One family may start its growth and development in the more informal family support center and progress to the more formal objective-driven family investment center. If the services operated by the two types of centers are well-coordinated, if cross-referrals are easy for families, and if collaborative planning is on-going at the community level, different models result in choice for families, not duplication.

Accountability.

Finally, Maryland sought and received funding from the Ford Foundation to support the creation of an accountability system—a Unified Family Service Information System. This local integrated data system will be both an outcome-oriented accountability system as well as a case-management tool. The system has four components: a family service history, a family fiscal account, a counselor's case-management tool, and a data networking capacity to eliminate duplication and to improve service effectiveness.

Maryland plans to feed information from this system into a proposed state-level integrated data system that creates client files over time, across all major state agencies. The data on clients will integrate assessment, history, eligibility, referrals, prevention efforts, and services (including home-based, institution-based, or outpatient) by their unique identifiers.

Iowa

In 1987 the Iowa General Assembly directed the Iowa Department of Human Services (IDHS) to develop a decategorized child welfare financing system in two counties in the state.[48] The desired outcomes were prevention of out-of-home placement and strengthened family functioning. The strategic path to be tried was an integrated system of serving children based on child and family needs rather than funding streams, prevention rather than crisis response, and intensive and flexible community-based services.

The Iowa legislature reviewed existing programs and practices. Their legislation mandated the creation of the following new components.

State level policy/program coordination.

The IDHS had responsibility for further developing and overseeing the initiative, but was directed to work with a statewide committee composed of representatives from all sectors of the child welfare system.

Employment/incentives for local integrated services.

As in the Maryland strategy, an incentive was constructed, offering the county use of "savings" from this more effective approach to support new or expanded children's services—a powerful incentive when coupled with overall budget neutrality. The usual pattern is for unexpended funds to return to the state and for localities to request new state funds for additional programs. Under the new arrangement, localities could benefit directly from efficiencies, using the funding according to their priorities (e.g., preventive services). Second, IDHS was directed to waive for the chosen counties any state regulations that could impede integrated services designed to accomplish the desired outcomes. The request for application from the counties stipulated that the application had to be signed jointly by the county board of supervisors, juvenile district court, and county department of human services. Fourth, technical assistance and support to the counties was provided by both the state and the foundation community. The Edna McConnell Clark Foundation supported full-time project coordinators in both counties.

Multiple models for local integrated services.

While guidance and technical assistance were offered, all decisions on services integration design were left up to the two counties. Planning was time-intensive. County professionals from social service agencies, from the county office of IDHS, and from the juvenile court, as well as private nonprofit providers, advocates, and private funders (e.g., United Way) had to get to know each other and to reach agreement on problems, goals, objectives, strategies, and implementation plans.

Although no statewide model was offered, the original county efforts have several common components: a pool of flexible funds for use by workers to provide services that could not be funded through traditional categorical services; a governance structure for these funds involving all key agencies; an improved client-tracking system based on the family unit as opposed to the individual child; new services that filled particular service gaps for a number of families (e.g., family preservation, therapeutic foster care, or day treatment); and cross-agency, coordinated and integrated service approaches to high-cost families involved with a number of service systems. Finally, both counties have recognized that a structure for ongoing collaborative interagency planning and evaluation involving more than the original agency planning group (e.g., the school system) is critical.

Accountability.

Although the accountability system for Iowa is in its infancy, the counties are tracking several key indicators. One is county placement rates at the state training school and the state juvenile home. A second is identification of the total costs expended upon families whose children are involved in several systems, to compare eventually with the costs of meeting those families' needs with alternative approaches that are more community-based, family-oriented and, hopefully, less costly to the state.

A Caveat

The strategic paths chosen by Maryland and Iowa emphasize services integration at the local level. Their approaches explore how the state can facilitate such integration, demonstrate its effectiveness and cost-saving potential, and expand the strategies statewide. In fact, many examples exist of successful local integrated services projects. Some, such as Focus on Youth (Los Angeles), the Ventura County project (California), or KIDS (Kentucky), integrate social services with education to benefit particular student populations. Others concentrate intensive, integrated services for families at risk of child abuse and disintegration. There are excellent materials available describing these programs and the components that make them successful.[49] Before leaping to the conclusion that integrated services are the only answer, however, policymakers should consider several points.

First, isolated examples of successful, family-oriented, local integrated programs do not constitute system reform. Without fundamental changes in how state and local agencies conduct business in providing services to people, these programs must constantly swim against a tide of federal and state categorical restrictions and disincentives to innovation. By themselves, they cannot make long-lasting and wide-scale improvements for families.

Second, while common components of local integrated services can be identified, local determination is the most critical element. State team leaders involved in CGPA's Family Policy Academy identified only seven core components in a potential state "request for proposal" to localities for implementing such services. These are:

- A local planning structure, some of whose members may be state prescribed by category—elected local official, county judge, or school superintendent, for example—but most of whom are selected by the locality itself

- A local governance structure for program operation, once planning has been completed, which is locally determined

- A set of criteria couched in broad, general language (e.g., comprehensive, culturally relevant, integrated, responsive) for the services to be provided to families

- An accountability system that tracks family outcomes, as well as services and costs, for entire families

- A service that refers families to other services in the community and/ or brokers these for them

- A single family record with at least a cover sheet common across all relevant agencies

- The capability of providing—depending upon the target family—a single or lead case manager; a single, cross-agency family assessment; home-based services; and outreach

Third, and most important, systems reform and local integrated services are only a means to an end—positive changes in the lives of people. For policymakers, attention can easily be distracted by the elegance of collaboration, communication systems, performance audits, and reorganizations. If these do not result in concrete, measurable improvements for families, we will have only stirred the pot, not enriched the meal. An alternative solution, not yet tried on a broad scale, would be to teach families how to negotiate "the system," as opposed to redesigning the system for them.

Although they are becoming clearer about what works to integrate services for families, state policymakers have encountered persistent difficulty in translating successful local programs into a statewide effort with broad-scale effect. Another step in overcoming this difficulty is to rethink state roles and responsibilities.

Think Beyond Old Roles and Responsibilities

State governments typically act as regulators, funders, and service providers. The strategies developed by Maryland and Iowa cast the Governor, cabinet officials, and agency staff in new roles.

Partner more than director.

Policymakers begin to act more as partners than directors when they define families functionally; when they develop a long range view of the family's functioning in a community context; when they capture the interrelationship of family strengths and problems; and when they envision solutions that involve actions on the part of individuals and families, as well as public and private programs and funding streams. Arkansas, Colorado, Iowa, Illinois, New York, Maryland, Oregon, Texas, and Washington—the ten participants in CGPA's Policy Academy—have envisioned state government as a partner with others in improving outcomes for families. Colorado's Family Policy Document states this most directly:

> *Colorado is ready to make significant reforms in the way it serves families and children. Yet, such reform can be accomplished only when all aspects of society (state and local government, business, funders, and private citizens) recognize the importance of families and children as the key to economic and social productivity.*[50]

Partnership has risks. In the role of partner, policymakers must be willing both to invest and ask for investment from others; to share control over key decisions (e.g., who should be helped, how much should be spent and under what circumstances, and how success is defined); share responsibility for success or failure; and recognize the strengths and accept the weaknesses of one's fellow partners. While executive policymakers may be used to sharing power with some (e.g., legislators), they may not be with others, such as local elected officials or community leadership. Sharing major decisions can be difficult for state policymakers, especially if some decisions are controlled by others not in the partnership (e.g., eligibility decisions in federally funded programs). Finally, sharing responsibility for failure may not be legally possible. In spite of these obstacles, partnership with the business community, foundations, and local governments (both county and city) is being vigorously pursued by Governors and other state officials.

Leader more than manager.

Warren Bennis defines managers as people who do things right. Leaders are people who do the right thing.[51] State policymakers must act as leaders if family policy is to be designed and implemented. Examples of this leadership drawn from the CGPA academy experience include:

- A Governor who insists that five agency heads make joint decisions on priority outcomes and programs for families and children in the face of limited resources

- A cabinet official who gently but persistently helps feuding program directors to understand each other's point of view and structures funding arrangements so that both can win

- An agency director who sticks his neck out to call other agency heads together to discuss possible action on a common agenda

- Agency senior staff who press forward on an interagency collaborative agenda in the absence of encouragement from the Governor's office

- Cabinet officials who attend public forums and regional meetings to offer new ideas and to listen as potential barriers are raised

- Members of interagency councils and commissions who one year following the end of a formal policy initiative continue to negotiate with federal officials to remove regulatory barriers, negotiate with each other on legislative and budget priorities, create a cross-agency children's program budget, blend categorical program funds for local projects, and set measurable outcome indicators for an accountability system on which they will be tracked

These leaders decided that real information is more useful than surface facts, that joint priority-setting is more powerful than protecting a line item, and that consensus yields better results than a behind-the-scenes deal. In short, these leaders decided that improving outcomes for families was more important than "turf."

Contractor more than provider.

Typically, the public sector has provided direct service in education, income assistance/welfare reform, child protection, and health and nutrition for low-income individuals. Services in employment and training, mental health, and substance abuse prevention and treatment have been indirect, contracted out by the public sector to private not-for-profit providers. While education, mental health, and employment and training services have been largely locally controlled, the state has controlled welfare reform, child protection, and public health and substance abuse services.

State policymakers are moving more services away from direct provision toward performance-based contracting and privatization. In addition, they are considering granting more control to local governance structures. Several challenges confront these leaders. First, policymakers must articulate clearly the results or expected outcomes to the contractor, company, or locality. Second, they must be skilled in designing accountability systems and reporting mechanisms that are timely, responsive and tied to consequences that can be implemented in a political environment. In the role of contractor, state officials act more as consultants, providing quality training and technical assistance to those who are delivering services with greater discretion. Finally, policymakers must listen and be responsive to those both providing and receiving service.

Quality assurer more than accountant.

The public sector is justifiably concerned with its legal obligations. Often this approach translates into concern over proper process. The state policymakers pioneering family policy have set their sights on quality outcomes, not just legal procedure. Although the task of establishing accountability systems based on outcomes is formidable, several states have begun to move forward. Chapter Five will detail this approach. In the business world, a quality product that meets customers' needs is a hallmark of "excellence." Public-sector leaders are beginning to define exactly what this term means as it relates to their investment in human resources.

Select and Plan

After developing and estimating costs for key strategies, and reviewing their roles and responsibilities, policymakers can select the best approaches based on the criteria of plausibility and feasibility.

Plausibility

Let's explore the concept of plausibility in relation to family policy. Continuing with our goal of family sustenance/healthy babies, a Governor is considering three strategic paths: prenatal care, promotion of healthy lifestyle choices, and the prevention of unplanned pregnancies. On what evidence are these strategies likely to succeed? Policymakers look for evidence from research, expert opinion, common sense, and consensus based on experience—also known as conventional wisdom.

Research supports the link between prenatal health services and healthier babies. But experts caution that obstetrical visits and medical services are not enough for young women with multiple risk factors. For these women, comprehensive services that link medical care with social, psychological, and financial support result in healthier babies.

Research also supports the effectiveness of health education and prevention services in causing healthier lifestyles and fewer high-risk behaviors, but for some populations, education must be coupled with service delivery. For example, some young women learn better nutrition by practicing cooking more nutritious meals. Pregnancy prevention is more likely if teens have ready access to contraceptives at the time they receive information.

On the basis of the above information, the Governor can safely conclude that all three strategic paths are plausible. A health promotion campaign, coupled with improved access to prenatal health services, will likely lead to healthier babies born to women from all incomes and family structures. Integrated health, social, psychological, and financial services are likely to improve birth outcomes for pregnant women in high risk circumstances.

There is considerable research linking integrated health and social services to improved family outcomes.[52] Less is known about the efficacy of linking social services to education. Many local, integrated services projects for high risk families have not been in existence long enough for research to be definitive.

Perfect information does not exist, but educated guesses on the plausibility of particular strategies can be made.

Feasibility

Many plausible strategies are not feasible. When considering feasibility, a range of factors should be considered: funding, time, leadership, and political capital. Implementation of the three strategic paths in our example requires extensive collaboration among state agencies—notably health, mental health, substance abuse prevention, education, Medicaid, welfare, child welfare, employment and training, and labor. A partnership with the business community is also likely to be necessary. Such collaboration will require leadership from the Governor, top cabinet officials and business. Developing and implementing a well-coordinated strategy may take two years and at least one legislative session. Political capital will have to be expended to encourage collaboration, gaining business support, and involving local communities and service providers.

Increasingly, Governors must estimate feasibility at both state and local levels. As counties and communities are required or encouraged by the state to implement integrated services delivery, local matching funds, time, leadership, and political capital are required. Attention should be given to the differences in capacity among metropolitan areas, regional centers, and rural areas and the differing amounts of support required.

Governors and their staffs should also consider such factors as the Governor's leadership style, the current level of public awareness on the issue, the anticipated level of opposition to proposed strategies, short- and longer-term state and local fiscal conditions, and the working relationship between the Governor and key legislative leadership. A solid feasibility analysis can help the Governor choose among or appropriately sequence several strategies. In our example, the Governor began by piloting integrated services to high-risk families in targeted communities, then she launched a high profile health education campaign. Once public awareness was raised and the business community was involved, she planned to develop a financing package to increase access to pregnancy prevention and prenatal health care services.

Plan for Implementation

When strategic paths are chosen, implementation planning can proceed. The implementation process is especially critical for family and children's policy, as it involves many agencies, sectors, and jurisdictions. Besides understanding the components of the plan, policymakers must consider the people who are involved in the planning. The greater the discretion required from those implementing the policy, the greater the importance of their involvement in planning. An implementation plan is more likely to yield results if it has the following components:

Major tasks.

The implementation plan should outline all major tasks in one document, illustrating how they fit together. For example, the major tasks in implementing integrated services pilots include (a) state level interagency policy coordination, (b) state and local community planning, (c) analysis and removal of regulatory barriers to sharing information among agencies and barriers to integrated services delivery, and (d) state budget reconfiguration to create a flexible funding pool. These activities should be coordinated with those for the statewide health education campaign, which could include focus groups with families from all income levels and cultural backgrounds, and planning meetings with advocates, program planners, and media experts. A third major task might be the formation of a Governor-appointed Blue Ribbon Commission on Family Health involving business and labor leaders.

Timing.

The plan should lay out broad time frames for major tasks. At a glance, policymakers should be able to see how the planning and implementation phases of each major component relate to the state's overall planning, budgeting, and legislative cycles; to agency program calendars; and to critical community events. Activities should be scheduled so that they reinforce, rather than conflict with, each other. For example, the recommendations of the Blue Ribbon Commission should be released during the health promotion campaign. The health promotion campaign should be timed to support the integrated services pilots in the high-risk communities.

Responsible agencies or individuals.

CGPA has found it useful to distinguish between those who have lead responsibility for implementation of a key component—those who are held accountable for its accomplishment—and those who have supporting responsibility. For example, the departments of health, education, and social services all may have responsibility for the design of the statewide media campaign on health education, but the director of the division of Maternal and Child Health may be held accountable for its success. Some plans also include the names of individuals or agencies who should be consulted or informed, or from whom approval is needed.

Expected outcomes.

Implementation plans should specify expected outcomes for each major activity. These outcomes are often the only short-term accountability mechanism available to a Governor who is relying on interagency, collaborative implementation. What are reasonable outcomes for the health education campaign? Choices include greater public awareness or reported behavior change as measured by surveys, a greater number of prenatal health care visits in targeted geographic areas, and a significant number of participating media markets or schools in partnership with community agencies.

This chapter has presented an approach to creating and selecting strategies for improving outcomes for families and children. Rather than offer a laundry list of relevant categorical programs or a summary of successful local integrated services projects, the chapter urges policymakers to think strategically, to collaborate on new activities and combinations of programs and services, and to support invention and collaboration at the local level. The Governor and other leaders are encouraged to rethink roles and responsibilities and to strengthen their ability to hold themselves and others accountable for quality results.

Family and children's policy is complex. Its implementation necessitates interagency, public, private, and multijurisdictional collaboration. Careful research and analysis and a persistent focus on family outcomes is needed to support the final selection and design of key strategies. Thoughtful implementation planning is just the beginning. To be successful, the Governor and cabinet officials must have a plan for ensuring accountability and gaining support over the long term.

Chapters Five and Six discuss these critical elements of the implementation plan.

CHAPTER FIVE:
GAUGING RESULTS

Now that you've decided what to do, how will you know whether you've done it? You might point to dollars spent, services provided, or even the number of people served. But will the answers tell you how people's lives have changed or how well families are doing?

Gauging the progress of your initiative by observing changes in family well-being is called performance accountability. A well-structured performance accountability system helps you understand what effect you are having as a result of the many initiatives taken on behalf of families.

The Governor in the story preceding Chapter Two asked pointed questions about families. Her policy director and agency heads worked together to develop a system to provide answers. They pulled information from a variety of sources in order to present a picture of how well families were functioning. The assessment viewed key indicators of family well-being, from some point in history up to the present. An accountability system monitors these indicators into the future in order to gauge change.

For a family initiative, you want to know about changes in people's lives, most particularly, those changes that strengthen or weaken the family. These may be changes in behavior, family circumstances, knowledge, skills, or even community conditions. Performance accountability systems can be developed, for instance, to track whether children's readiness for school improves in states where funding for preschool programs has been increased, whether fewer at-risk youth run away from home in communities that operate well-attended youth programs, whether those who complete job training programs obtain good jobs, or whether more low-income families live in decent housing this year than last.

A performance accountability system provides the framework for measuring family outcomes, not merely agency processes or workloads. The information it provides can be used effectively by policymakers and program managers. The system feeds information back to policymakers and program managers so that they can not only gauge the success of their efforts, but also adjust policies and programs when needed. A performance accountability system also can provide program providers useful information about the effect of their service. Consumers of services can use the information to choose among services. And the public— the state's stockholders—is better informed about the "value of their stock."

This chapter summarizes the important elements of performance accountability. Adapted from a companion CGPA volume, *Getting Results*, by Jack Brizius and Michael Campbell, this chapter answers the following questions:

- What is performance accountability ?
- Why develop an accountability system for family policy?
- What are the key components of the system?
- What are its limitations?

What Is Performance Accountability?

A performance accountability system looks at results: Are families better off now than they were last year? Other management and reporting systems look at "inputs" or "processes" of human service systems: the number of people served, costs of service, how closely procedures are followed, whether standards of quality are met, or whether expenditures track budgets. These mechanisms might reveal how efficiently the system is run, but they say little about whether family circumstances have improved. Performance accountability holds the system responsible for producing certain changes in the lives of those it serves. It combines a look at broad policy outcomes (policy accountability) and results of specific programs (program accountability).

Policy accountability focuses on whether a complex set of state programs and actions are achieving broad goals and objectives. Individual programs might fail while overall policies succeed. Conversely, a program might be strong while larger problems persist. For this reason, policy accountability looks at outcomes for whole groups or classes of people, not just for those who have taken part in particular programs. It measures the effect of regulatory and tax policy, as well as the set of programs related to the problem. The outcomes are interpreted in the context of the entire state system and its prevailing political and economic conditions, and it compares performance on agreed-upon objectives over time.

Program accountability measures specific program outcomes. It tracks only those served by the program. It stays focused on the program's objectives. Measures and standards of performance are derived from individual program outcome statements. These specify, in quantifiable terms, the changes desired in individual behavior or circumstances as a result of program interventions. Outcome data are interpreted primarily as they relate to specific programs or program components. These can include numbers served, cost of service, measures of the quality of service, the sequence of services, and other measures.

Both types of accountability systems focus on outcomes for individuals or families as the measure of performance. Both must be built into the policymaking and program development process from the beginning. Thinking about accountability helps structure the policymaking process from the moment of problem identification and assessment. In Chapter Two we focused on assessing the well-being of families. As a starting point we had to decide what we mean by family well-being and what indicators tell us about families. Performance accountability causes us to ask, "If families were better off, how would we know? What would they be achieving? What would indicate that this is or is not happening?" The answers to these questions become the outcomes to monitor and the measures to use.

Why Develop an Accountability System for Your Family Initiative?

In most states, programs for families and children abound. They are housed in several state agencies, including health, social services, corrections, education, and community development. They account for more than half of the state's general fund expenditures. Beyond state government, there are hundreds of programs and services run by county and municipal governments, nonprofit family service agencies, church groups, chambers of commerce, and civic leagues. Determining the cumulative effect of all these programs and assessing the specific effect of the state's investment provides essential information to guide policy decisions in several ways.

First, you have a means for testing the basic premises driving your policy. For example, your policy may place an emphasis on restructuring services to be more integrated. The underlying premise is that integration would enhance access to services, make services more responsive to families, and thereby improve family outcomes. With a performance accountability system, you could determine whether the services are indeed more integrated and accessible. More importantly, you could then step back and ask whether people are better off as a result, providing a basis for checking your assumptions about the organization of services and their effect on outcomes. An accountability system also provides an opportunity to refine or redirect your strategy.

Second, performance accountability helps keep you on track. By systematically monitoring the progress of families and reporting outcomes on a regular basis, the focus stays on people and changes over time.

Third, performance accountability gives you more information with which to make crucial resource allocation decisions. Most Governors and legislators want better evidence of the results of policies and programs than are typically provided. Using selected performance measures, accountability systems produce timely estimates of what is working and what is not. This information allows Governors and legislators to feel more confident in making hard budget and resource allocation decisions.

Fourth, a performance accountability system creates incentives for service providers to improve performance. When you specify desired outcomes, monitor whether there is progress toward their achievement, and make management and budget decisions on the basis of results, the results you get are more likely to be positive.

Performance accountability can also greatly increase the willingness of program managers to experiment with new ways of meeting goals and objectives set by political leaders. If program managers know that political leaders are primarily interested in outcomes measured through a performance accountability system, they are more likely to innovate to achieve those outcomes. When the system is focused on the results of services instead of on the process of delivering services, state agency chiefs and program managers are less likely to stick to "standard operating procedure" in an effort to protect themselves from criticism if something goes wrong.

Performance accountability is a good idea for other reasons as well:

- It responds to a growing public concern about the ability of government to deliver solid results. Voters and taxpayers want proof that policies and programs are working, and judging from the low turnout at the polls and strong resistance to tax hikes, they are not at all convinced.

- It can give political leaders "good news" about policies and programs that enable them to take credit for success, and it can warn them of "bad news" early on.

- It can speed the rate at which innovations spread throughout a human services system, because successful practices will show up in reports to political leaders.

Finally, allocating resources on the basis of performance can free both policymakers and service providers from the necessity of specifying through rules and regulations exactly what providers must do. In this sense, accountability systems can provide the basis for a new way of governing—through the measurement of performance rather than through the bureaucratic process.

What Are the Components of a Performance Accountability System?

A performance accountability system has three components: defining outcomes and performance standards, measuring performance, and reporting results.

Defining Outcomes and Performance Standards.

Outcomes are changes that occur as a result of events, conditions, and/or circumstances. In this case, they are the changes that you hope will occur if your policy is successful. In defining outcomes for a performance accountability system it is important to determine not only what the change will be, but also, whose lives will change, how much, and by when. Such an outcome might be stated as follows: "By 1995, the infant mortality and low birth-weight rates for babies of low-income women will improve by 25 percent."

Performance standards are realistic estimates of expected outcomes. They should be easily understood and agreed to by both those who will judge the success of policies and programs and those who will be held accountable. The most realistic standards usually have been jointly developed by these two groups. In setting standards, many factors may be taken into account: the amount of resources deployed, the baseline skill levels or problems of those served, the intensity of a service or treatment, or the power of the incentives that are used to produce changes. As a result, performance standards may vary greatly for seemingly similar programs or even for the same program operating in different parts of a state.

Setting performance standards is one of the most challenging tasks in establishing a performance accountability system, and it is undoubtedly the most controversial. Standards must not be set so high that a policy or program has no chance of being judged a success. On the other hand, standards must be ambitious enough to motivate those responsible for meeting the standards to do their best.

Measuring Performance.

A clearly defined outcome can be translated easily into a measurable performance indicator. In the above example, the indicators are infant mortality rates and birth weight data. Collecting data on these two indicators on a regular basis will reveal whether birth outcomes are changing. Indicators are usually proxies for what we really want to measure. Selection of indicators that most nearly match the measures we are seeking is an extremely important part of the process. In Chapter Two we discussed selecting indicators that relate to family well-being when conducting your assessment. These same indicators become your baseline for accountability. It is important to select a few good indicators. The data should be gathered on a regular basis (e.g., quarterly or yearly), and the same data should be collected each time in order to make comparisons.

It is often necessary to use a variety of indicators to estimate a single outcome. Each indicator may reveal only partial information about the outcome we really want to measure. Just as student attendance is only one aspect of a healthy school, many outcome indicators are only a partial measurement of the desired outcome.

Reporting Results.

Given its wide-ranging value, the information will be reported in a number of ways. Program management summaries will be prepared in the agencies. The budget or planning office usually will prepare reports for senior staff and policymakers, as well as for political leaders. The Governor's communications office should be involved in preparing accountability information for release to the public and press.

Reports will differ in form and extent, depending on the audience. They should all be designed to be read rapidly, to be based on summary information, to use graphics to convey substantial amounts of information, and to exhibit varying degrees of analysis. Some reports give just the facts. Others attempt to draw conclusions on the basis of analysis of patterns in the data. Whether or not state officials want to attempt to use an accountability system to provide the basis for analysis depends on the degree of reliability of the data, how the publication of the data will be perceived, and whether or not the analysis is timely.

Limitations of Performance Accountability Systems

Performance accountability systems may be able to estimate the outcomes of programs and policies and to monitor change, but they cannot determine the true impact of programs and policies on people. To measure the effectiveness of particular interventions, it is necessary to undertake experiments that involve program groups and control groups developed through random assignment. The impact of interventions on the program group are calculated using the outcomes for the control group as a benchmark for comparison. However, because this type of experiment is both difficult and expensive, it is seldom used as a management tool.

In addition, performance accountability systems cannot be used directly to determine the success or failure of a policy or program. An accountability system designed for an adult basic skills program, for example, may measure improvement in the reading levels of clients, as well as the number of hours of computer-based instruction and hours of individual tutoring received. Without a controlled study and direct measurements, however, program managers will not be able to determine with certainty whether tutoring or computer-based instruction is more effective in teaching reading. An accountability system may tell policymakers and program managers that participants in a particular youth employment program are obtaining and keeping jobs, but it will not tell them whether the program is responsible for the success or whether an upsurge in the local economy has caused the labor market to tighten.

Accountability systems are also limited by the accuracy of the outcome measures selected and the quality of the data collected. In most cases there are no readily available performance indicators that are truly accurate measures of desired outcomes. As a result, accountability systems most often use "proxies" for the data that we really want to collect. Designers of the accountability system may warn others that these proxies do not actually measure the true outcomes, but by the time the information reaches policymakers and senior managers, these caveats may be lost or ignored. Policy decisions and program modifications may then be based on incomplete or misleading information. There are ways to guard against these dangers, but the use of misleading data can be devastating to a policy or program, especially if information is used prematurely.

Finally, just as accountability systems can provide incentives for improving program operations and for changing the behavior of service providers, they can provide perverse incentives as well. The managers of programs designed to place welfare recipients in jobs, for example, may find that their own performance is measured by job placement rates. As a result, they may push recipients into jobs requiring low skills before they have had a chance to acquire skills that will result in long-term placements. The unintended consequence may be to put welfare recipients right back into the low-skill, low-wage job market from which they dropped into welfare in the first place.

As with positive incentives, perverse incentives will be stronger if accountability systems are linked to resource allocation, but they will be present even if there is no direct link between published information and budgets. Making sure that the implementation of an accountability system does not produce perverse incentives is an important part of designing an effective system.

Conclusion

By comparing actual achievements to established standards, accountability systems can serve as report cards for estimating the performance of family policies and programs. They are also excellent management tools for keeping human services administrators and workers focused on producing positive changes in people's lives. Accountability systems do not provide a way to judge with certainty the effectiveness of policies or programs. To do this requires rigorous controlled studies (e.g., impact evaluations) that compare the outcomes for groups that have received services to the outcomes for similar groups that have not.

CHAPTER SIX:
GAINING SUPPORT

Big changes in the way states conduct business don't happen easily or often. There are times, however, when such change is needed. In the case of human services, for many states that time has come. Critics decry the current system's lack of results, pointing to inhumane treatment, inappropriate services, and a disjointed approach. They argue for a system that is seamless, integrated, linked with communities, and, most of all, responsive to families.

Change is inherently difficult; it threatens the security of people and institutions. In the organization of human services, given how large and complex these institutions are, a minor change can take a lot of time. What's worse, some hard-fought-for symbols of change in a political environment—reorganizations, special commissions, newly formed agencies—can be superficial, masking the fact that things are the same.

What does it take to make things really change? It takes many people understanding that the change is for the better. For a family initiative to work, it takes the actions of hundreds, if not thousands, of players (consumers and providers of services, as well as those who establish the rules) who feel it is in their own interest, and in the interest of others, to do things differently.

This chapter is about gaining support for change. It discusses why you should focus on support as you develop your initiative. It presents a way of thinking about gaining support. And it presents several principles to help guide you as you develop policies in your state.

Why Be Concerned About Gaining Support?

A policy initiative to strengthen families relies on the actions of a multitude of players. It will require participation from those who have an obvious interest—families, community leaders, child and family advocates, service providers, county and state agencies. It also requires participation from those whose interest is less obvious, such as business and union leaders, and champions of other causes. Each of these players will make choices, which individually and collectively contribute to the overall success or failure of the initiative. Families choose to participate in programs when they are confident that doing so will improve their lives. Innovative service providers, like business entrepreneurs, choose to invest time and resources in designing new programs when they are certain that their approach will enjoy community support. State and county agencies will integrate services more effectively if they believe that doing so will improve the quality of both the services and their professional lives. Businesses will adopt policies that are more family-oriented if employers and employees understand that it will pay off. Taxpayers are willing to invest in the initiative if they are certain that the investment will result in better schools, safer streets, healthier babies, and more housing.

Building support for your policy initiative is no simple matter. Those who have a stake in the future of families and children have strong views regarding what should happen and how. Each service provider, whether it is the state welfare agency or the church-run homeless shelter, has its own structure, system, and culture—all of which resist change. All are concerned about money and turf, and they worry about shifting the balance. Moreover, you must gain support from a variety of players over whom you have little control. Those whose interests are less immediate are difficult to engage. They need to be convinced that what benefits families at risk benefits them as well.

Perhaps the most difficult aspect of gaining support is that your family initiative represents a sea change for which there is no ground swell. It is a new way of doing business that views the family as the critical unit for policy and challenges institutions inside and outside of government to behave differently. At the same time, these changes are not occurring in response to an impassioned public outcry for reform. Most people do not see themselves as part of a family at risk and, therefore, do not share the sense of urgency. Education reform, by contrast, is more widespread because everyone with children or grandchildren wants quality education.

Hard as it may be to build support for the initiative, it will be harder if you don't. Your assessment of the problems, opportunities, and strategy might be limited or off target without the broad perspective others bring. You may not be able to marshall the level of investment needed to carry out the initiative. You may spend a great deal of time designing and building a product that your customers—families and children—do not value or use.

Moreover, if you fail to include those who have a stake in the policy, they may undermine the initiative down the road. A family initiative relies on many people dedicated to achieving the same results, all contributing in their unique way. Because it is decentralized, diffuse, and not easily controlled, the initiative needs widespread support.

How To Think About Gaining Support

Developing a policy initiative is much like marketing a product. In the private sector, marketing involves two elements: merchandising and promotion.[53]

Merchandising is what you do to determine what the product should be. The company invests in learning what people want to buy. Then the company makes it. As William Nothdurft, writer and policy advisor, stated: "In the public sector, policy merchandising is the art of knitting the interests, hopes, and dreams of the customers into the crafting of a public policy product. There are no objectively correct policies or programs; the needs, beliefs, hopes and dreams of the people who live and work in a community determine what kinds of initiatives can succeed."[54]

Promotion is what you do to sell the product. It is done in two stages. The first involves promoting the product idea to investors—the stockholders. They need to be certain that the product will be profitable. In the public sector, the stockholders include all potential investors—the general public, state and local officials, community leaders, neighborhood service providers, foundation and business executives. Profitability in the public sector translates into quality of life: good schools, safe streets, economic opportunity, and easy access to quality services. These facets may be tougher to measure than bottom-line corporate profits, but they are what counts when it comes to votes, taxes, and support for new initiatives.

The second stage involves promoting the product to customers. They want to see that it meets their needs and conforms to their tastes. In the private and public sectors, promotion requires developing a crisp message that conveys the essence of the product and captures consumer interest. It also involves determining when, where, and how to present the message. Gaining support entails the careful weaving of the needs, hopes, and tastes of customers—children and families— with the motivations and interests of investors, in the making of public policy. While there are no fixed rules to guarantee success, the following principles have served many state leaders well.

Principles of Merchandising Family Policy

Identify the Range of Interests.

Identifying the range of interests is an important early step in gaining support. Doing so reveals a great deal about the breadth and depth of concerns related to your policy initiative.

While there are any number of ways to organize the analysis, we recommend asking two basic questions: Who is, or should be, interested, and what motivates their interest?

Determine the Customers for This Product.

Are the customers families and children exclusively, or are there others? Are our categories too broad? What are the subsets? What do we know about their tastes and preferences? How do we know that they would prefer something other than the products that are now on the market? Do they want different services, or the same services improved?

To find out about customer preferences, it is helpful to involve the "target market." Observe how services are currently utilized. Discover what families think of these services. What do they value most? What doesn't work? What is missing? Convene families in focus groups, hold hearings, ask communities to work with you to organize town meetings or conduct survey interviews. Involve families and service providers and compare responses.

Washington State is developing an initiative to assure that services are relevant to families. They have identified a broad vision for that service delivery system; It should be family focused, culturally relevant, coordinated, and locally planned. They refer to their merchandising plan as "ownership development."

They are convening fifty focus groups involving customers (e.g., children in one, parents in another, teachers in another). They want customer views on the vision— what do they like and dislike about it? They want to know what is missing. They want to know how they think the service delivery system should look.

Identify Likely Investors.

This list might include the legislature, budget director, agency directors, county and city executives and councils, foundations, corporate and union leaders, and all taxpayers. What kind of product will motivate them to invest? Are they dissatisfied with what is currently produced? Why?

Consider Who Else You Need To Help Merchandise and Develop the Product.

These might include agency and program directors at the state, county, and community levels. They would include schools, the public, and nonprofit and private service providers. They also might include opinion makers in the media and well-known civic leaders. What are their interests? What product would inspire them? Why would they want to help coordinate the overall production process, enhance the quality of the current product, and/or embrace new ones?

Develop a Profile of Competitors and Opponents.

This list could include service providers who are uncomfortable with change, or agency and program directors who see the initiative as a threat. It might include other related initiatives, sparked by a foundation or business group's wanting to be recognized as the principal change agent. It might include advocates for other issues (e.g., transportation, environment) who want to be certain of their share of the budget. You will want to consider what distinguishes your products from theirs. Will the family initiative be an addition to, a replacement for, or a refinement of existing products? You will want to know more about the nature of their opposition to the new product, where you can find common ground, and where you are likely to agree to disagree.

Principles of Promoting Family Policy

Start at the Top.

The Governor is uniquely positioned to lead the charge. He can raise awareness, set the terms of the debate, present a vision, and generate enthusiasm unlike any other state official. The Governor, through his public addresses, press interviews, and meetings with business and community leaders, can call attention to families. He can generate public understanding of the issues, dispel myths, and communicate realistic expectations.

The Governor can make connections—showing how strengthening families relates to other important economic and social goals. Governor Schaefer of Maryland argues that everything else is subordinate to investing in families. He makes the case that, unless Maryland rests on a foundation of strong, healthy, capable families, it will be difficult to make needed economic and environmental gains.

The Governor can gather together his agency heads to direct their efforts in support of families. He can convene potential investors and customers—parents and children, business and union leaders, philanthropists, opinion makers, service providers—introduce ideas, focus their attention, and hear their views. Colorado Governor Roy Romer and First Lady Bea Romer are convening nine regional forums for the general public. Cosponsored by the State Commission on Families and Children, the Decade of the Child Coalition, and the Public Service Company of Colorado, these forums are for the purpose of sharing the state's draft on family initiative for comment. Each of these nine regions uses a community steering committee to organize its forum and focus on its concerns.

While it is neither practical nor desirable for the Governor to be the only spokesperson for families, it is the Governor's priority. Others inside and outside of the administration will make a persuasive case for a family policy. It helps if they are reinforced by the Governor's message.

Begin Early.

To have an effect, the Governor must be eager to speak up early and often. Creating broad-based support for a new policy direction can be slow and plodding. People must see how the initiative will serve their interests. They need to grasp how it affects their community and their lives.

Governor Clinton of Arkansas talked about families well before all the pieces of his policy initiative were crafted. During the campaigns and throughout his tenure as Governor, he has taken every opportunity to draw attention to the importance of strengthening families. He made connections with people's lives. He said repeatedly that the challenges facing families are not solely reserved for those in poverty. He uses examples of biases against working mothers with preschool children to drive the point home.

Determine How and When to Involve the Players.

It is unlikely that you will involve all the players in the same way at once. This would be neither practical nor productive. Nor is it likely that you will identify all the interests in the first round of analysis. New ones will develop as you move along. The process of gaining support is ongoing and must be flexible enough to involve new participants along the way.

During the early stages of policy development, you will want to generate enthusiasm for the concepts and refine the ideas. You will want to be sure that a base of support for the initiative is developing. Once the policy initiative takes shape, you will want broad-based confirmation and support. Throughout implementation, you will need the active participation of many. They need to grasp and support the purpose of the policy, have a clear understanding of their role, and be motivated to contribute to its success.

Consider the composition of the core team for policy development. Does this team reflect the range of interests? If not, how will you ensure that the full range is embraced in the process? There are a number of ways to do this. The policy development team can meet with "customers" and "investors" in town meetings around the state at key points throughout the process. Focus groups, hearings, and survey interviews can also effectively bring in a broader range of interests.

In Maryland, the Special Secretary for Children, Youth, and Families spearheaded the effort on behalf of the Governor. At every turn she took the work of the subcabinet out to the community for comment. She joined private service providers at their regular meetings. She attended parent groups. She invited parents, service providers, and community leaders to meet with the subcabinet. She briefed legislative leaders regularly. Not only did her effort to communicate help to build support, it greatly enriched the work of the subcabinet.

In Colorado, Governor Romer and members of his cabinet conducted briefings for 365 state employees to solicit their comments on the draft plan. Cabinet members and county officials convened ten county social services forums, and more than 100 briefings with service and professional organizations for the same purpose.

Blue ribbon panels and task forces can be created. It is essential that you recognize that these groups are most effective when their charge is specific and clear. They must be staffed sufficiently to do the job. Don't make the mistake of using them as a device to give the appearance of broad-based involvement. You must be serious, or the whole initiative will unravel.

Make the Message Simple and Compelling.

The message must hit home crisply. The complexities of your data assessment and policy analysis must translate into terms that relate to people's lives. Avoid "insider" phrases and technical terms. Nothdurft writes that brevity and simplicity is essential—not because people are stupid, they are not. It is because people are busy.[54]

The message should not be about process, but about product. What will the Governor point to three years from now, that will prove that families are better off? In building support for their comprehensive infant mortality initiative in Washington, D.C., district leaders worked with Jerry Wishnow of the Wishnow Group, to translate reams of technical reports, demographic and health statistics, complex goals and outcome objectives into the phrase "Beautiful babies right from the start."[55] This message is something everyone can relate to, everyone hopes for. People know what the product is. The message is clear, and it is human.

Deliver the Message Often.

Repetition is essential. An occasional speech or an occasional front page news story will not focus public attention or convince anyone that you are serious. Opportunities abound. Here are just a few:

- Focus the "State Of The State" message and other major addresses given by the Governor on the family initiative.

- Think strategically about the Governor's schedule. With the scheduling secretary, be systematic about building opportunities to speak to key stakeholders.

- Have the Governor and/or the commission on families or the policy development team visit local programs that reflect the direction the initiative will take. Ask community leaders to host the visit and draw media attention at every turn.

- Have recognition events for family initiatives, hold a Governor's conference on the family, or have a family celebration week with press conferences.

- Develop a media campaign. Arrange for the message to be repeated on television and radio during prime time. Have it be the topic of talk shows, news commentary, and documentaries, as well as public service announcements.

- Invite parents and children who are involved in successful family initiatives to join the Governor at national meetings such as those of the National Governors' Association. Notify the hometown paper that local children were recognized nationally.

Share Credit.

Because the success of the initiative relies on the good will and direct actions of so many, take every opportunity to bring attention to their contribution. Remember to mention others as a matter of course when being interviewed by the press, making presentations to the Kiwanis Club, or talking to a colleague on the phone. Be sure that promotional materials have names prominently displayed. Organize events to honor special contributors. By the time the initiative is ready to implement, many will feel "ownership," something that in a political environment often becomes a power-play, jockeying for party or candidate identification with the ideas. Try to turn this into a win/win, as opposed to a winner-take-all, situation. If you share credit wherever and whenever possible, it will invariably reflect well on you.

Keep the Initiative Visible.

Because this is a long-term proposition, it is unlikely that the issue will sustain an intensity of interest. Issues maintain center stage for a limited time. Make the most of it when you have center stage, and create opportunities to get on stage as the play progresses. One way to do this is to develop a systematic reporting of progress, like a "report card" on family well-being. Another is to have an annual event, like a family week or a regular Governor's conference on the family.

A Final Word

A strategy for gaining support, like marketing, involves risk. The more people you involve, the greater the chance of losing control. Those speaking on behalf of the initiative may promise too much or convey the wrong message. Hearings and town meetings could break down into gripe sessions. You may get mixed signals about what people want and how willing they are to embrace change. Early supporters may drop out over time. You may build expectations for results which exceed your ability to produce. Be prepared for setbacks. But remember, rarely do the risks outweigh the benefits. A far-reaching policy initiative for families and children cannot proceed in isolation. No matter how well conceived, its success depends upon the support of many.

EPILOGUE

It has been six years since the Governor announced her family initiative. Much has happened. The first assessment led to the development of a report card on family well-being, which is presented each year. The results point to increases in parental involvement in school. More children are entering school healthy and alert. More students are staying in high school, the graduation rate has increased slightly, and test scores have improved. More pregnant women are getting prenatal care, and the rate of infant mortality and low birth-weight babies has stabilized. But the rate of teens giving birth continues to rise.

Formerly absent fathers are playing a more active role in the care of their children, but the divorce and single-parent household rates persist at high levels. Neighborhoods have become communities. No longer do people turn their heads in the face of hunger, abuse, and neglect. Community members are involved in stamping out drugs, cleaning up playgrounds, organizing sports events, fixing up abandoned houses, and creating adult learning centers.

Rose graduated from high school and entered the state university with a scholarship. Michael has a job and is working on his associate degree. Ray left his old job for one that offered more flexibility and more pay. Maureen was able to cut back to a part-time job in order to spend more time with John. Ray's parents have moved into a supported living complex that accommodates their needs for intellectual stimulation, companionship, health care, and practical assistance in adapting to Ray's mother's deteriorating condition.

What accounts for these changes? While there are a number of forces contributing, one stands out. The state has become a place where families are important. The Governor spends a lot of time in communities, meeting with parents, kids, teachers, school principals, religious leaders, business and union leaders. She and her cabinet observed, in the early years, what happened when children arrived at school hungry and tired, what happened when poorly educated single parents tried to juggle a job search with raising children, what happened when dual-income families couldn't get the flexibility they needed to care for aging parents and

100

young children. They saw what happened when families were unable to get medical care for their children. And they watched how the state's human service systems responded.

They saw first-hand how the Roses, Michaels, Rays, and Maureens got bounced around from agency to agency. They saw little progress and lots of confusion.

The Governor's initiative was geared to make fundamental changes in the culture and routine of the human service delivery system. The new culture is rooted in the notion that families come first. All progress is measured by whether people's lives are improved. The system takes its lead from families, and families experience the system as friendly, responsive, and seamless.

Moreover, the state no longer defines itself as a "human services provider." The Governor's initiative positions the state to be a catalyst. The statewide commitment to families is a partnership, with an array of related public and private investments in the well-being of people. These investments have combined to upgrade housing, build community capacity, support entrepreneurs in poor communities, develop family centers, increase access to medical services, encourage variety and vitality in the public schools, spawn child care, and develop workplace literacy programs.

Looking back on her first term, the Governor readily admits the difficulty. There were conflicts over turf, over values, over resources, over program direction. There were seemingly intractable rules, regulations, and habits.

The recession cut the guts out of the state budget. In the face of the largest deficit known to the state, this initiative would, at best, redirect, not reduce, spending.

It was hard to cultivate a new way of thinking about families, and about the state role. Reinventing a system that is innovative, responsive to people, and enterprising is tough, and we still have a long way to go.

Of all the challenges, the most trying is patience. Real improvements in the lives of families could take a generation. "But," she says, "we have a renewed spirit in this state. We all have a sense of purpose and drive. We were able to rise to our best instincts and make a commitment to ourselves and to future generations, that our families will be strong."

ENDNOTES

1. This case was adapted from Bernard Lefkowitz, *Tough Change: Growing Up On Your Own In America*, (New York: The Free Press of Macmillan, Inc., 1987).

2. National Commission on Children, *Beyond Rhetoric: A New American Agenda For Children and Families*, (Washington, DC: National Commission on Children, 1991).

See also U.S. Department of Commerce, Bureau of the Census, *Current Population Reports*, ser. P-60, no. 168, *Money Income and Poverty Status in the United States: 1989* (Washington DC: Government Printing Office, 1990).

3. U.S. Department of Health and Human Services, National Center for Health Statistics, "Births, Marriages, Divorces and Deaths for 1991," *Monthly Vital Statistics Report 39*, no.7.

4. K.A. Moore, *Facts at A Glance* (Washington, DC: Child Trends, 1991).

5. Harold L. Hodgkinson, *The Same Client: The Demographics Of Education And Service Delivery Systems,* (Washington, DC: Institute for Educational Leadership, Inc/Center For Demographic Policy, 1989).

6. *Ibid*.

7. U.S. Department of Commerce, Bureau of the Census, *Current Population Reports,* ser. P-20, no. 447, *Household and Family Characteristics: March 1990 and 1989* (Washington, DC: Government Printing Office, 1990).

8. U.S. Department of Commerce, Bureau of the Census, *Current Population Reports,* ser. P-20, no.445, *Marital Status and Living Arrangements: March 1989* (Washington, DC: Government Printing Office, 1990).

9. Andrew J. Cherlin, Frank Furstenberg, Jr., P. Lindsay Chase-Lansdale, et al., "Longitudinal Studies of Effects of Divorce on Children in Great Britain and the United States," *Science*, 7 June 1991, p.1386-1389.

10. National Commission on Children, *Beyond Rhetoric*

11. U.S. Department of Commerce, Bureau of the Census, *Current Population Reports,* ser. P-70, no.20, *Who's Minding The Kids? Child Care Arrangements: 1986-87* (Washington, DC: Government Printing Office, 1990).

12. Family Support Act (Public Law 100-485).

13. Marcia A. Howard, *Fiscal Survey of the States, April 1991* (National Governors' Association/National Association of State Budget Officers, Washington D.C. 1991).

14. *The Sacramento Bee*, 9 Jan. 1990, Metro section B.

15. Dr. Gail Christopher, opening remarks, State Policy Academy on Families and Children at Risk, December 1989.

16. National Commission on Children, *Beyond Rhetoric*

17. From New York State Council on Children and Families, *State of the Child in New York State*. The report cites Census definition as Census Bureau, 1982b on p. 45 of the Report.

18. New York State Council, *State of the Child*

19. Lisbeth Schorr, *Within Our Reach: Breaking the Cycle of Disadvantage* (New York: Anchor Press, Doubleday, 1988), p.25.

20. Louise Flick, *Adolescent Childbearing Decisions: Implications for Prevention* (St. Louis: The Danforth Foundation, 1984).

21. Susan E. Foster, *Preventing Teenage Pregnancy: A Public Policy Guide* (Washington, DC: Council of State Policy and Planning Agencies, 1986), p.35-42.

22. U.S. Department of Education, Office of Educational Research and Improvement, *Dealing with Dropouts: The Urban Superintendents' Call to Action* (Washington, DC: U.S. Government Printing Office, Nov. 1987), p.5.

23. William Julius Wilson, *The Truly Disadvantaged, The Inner City, the Underclass, and Public Policy* (Chicago: The University of Chicago Press, 1987).

24. Margaret Wilkerson and Jewell Handy Gresham, "Sexual Politics of Welfare: The Racialization of Poverty," *The Nation*, 24/31 July 1989, vol. 249, no. 4, p. 126, 127.

25. Jay Belsky and Teresa Nezworski, *Clinical Implications of Attachment* (Hillsdale, New Jersey: Lawrence Erlbaum Associates, 1988).

26. Vonnie C. McLoyd, "The Impact of Economic Hardship on Black Families and Children: Psychological Distress, Parenting, and Socioemotional Development," *Child Development*, April 1990, vol. 61, no. 2, p. 311-346 (published by the Society for Research in Child Development, Inc.).

27. Gordon Berlin and Andrew Sum, *Toward A More Perfect Union* (New York: Ford Foundation, Feb. 1988), p.36.

28. *Ibid.*

29. *Ibid.*, p.39.

30. *Ibid.*, p.42.

31. Jewelle Taylor Gibbs, "The New Morbidity: Homicide, suicide, accidents, and life-threatening behaviors," *Young, Black, and Male in America: An*

Endangered Species, Ed. J.T. Gibbs (Dover, MA: Auburn House Publishing Company, 1988).

32. Michael E. Conner, "Teenage fatherhood: Issues Confronting Young Black Males," *Young, Black, and Male*, Ed. J.T. Gibbs, p.198.

33. Berlin and Sum, *Toward A More Perfect Union*, p.56.

34. Rodney J. Reed, "Education and Achievement of Young Black Males," *Young, Black, and Male*, Ed. J.T. Gibbs, p.82.

35. Albert Bandura and Dale H. Schunk, "Cultivating Competence, Self-Efficacy, and Intrinsic Interest through Proximal Self-Motivation," *Journal of Personality and Social Psychology*, 41: 586-598

36. Berlin and Sum, *Toward A More Perfect Union*, p.42-49.

37. William E. Nothdurft and Barbara R. Dyer, *Out From Under: Policy Lessons From A Quarter Century Of Wars On Poverty* (Washington, DC: Council of State Policy and Planning Agencies, January 1990).

38. *Panel Studies on Income Dynamics*, University of Michigan

39. Jerry Abboud, *A Permanent Home: The Issue of Children in Foster Care* (Washington, DC: National Council of State Legislators, March 1984).

Maryann Jones, *A Second Chance for Families—Five Years Later* (New York: Child Welfare League of America, 1985).

40. Andrew Hahn, Jacqueline Danzberger, and Bernard Lefkowitz, *Dropouts in America: Enough is Known for Action* (Washington, DC: Institute for Educational Leadership, 1987).

41. Schorr, *Within Our Reach*

42. Mark Testa and Edward Lawlor, *The State Of The Child: 1985*, (Chicago: The Chapin Hall Center for Children at The University of Chicago, 1985).

43. New York State Council, *State Of The Child*

44. Governor's Families and Children Initiative, Draft Community Report Card, 1991 (For more information, contact Donna Chitwood in the Office of Governor Roy Romer, Denver, Colorado).

45. Andrew J. Cherlin et al., "Longitudinal Studies"

46. Schorr, *Within Our Reach*, p.68-70.

47. J. David Hawkins, Ph.D. and Richard F. Catalano, Ph.D., "Risk and Protective Factor for Alcohol and Other Drug Problems in Adolescence and Early Adulthood," (unpublished manuscript), Social Development Research Group, School of Social Work, University of Washington, Seattle.

48. Charlie Bruner and Richard Flintrop, monograph on Child Welfare Collaborations, (published by Center for Social Policy, 1991).

49. Martin Blank and Atelia I. Melaville, *What it Takes: Structuring Interagency Partnerships to Connect Children and Families with Comprehensive Services* (Education and Human Services Consortium, Institute for Education Leadership, 1991).

50. State of Colorado's unpublished report on its participation in the Policy Academy on Families and Children At Risk, conducted by the Council of Governors' Policy Advisors (Washington, D.C.).

51. Warren Bennis, *Why Leaders Can't Lead* (San Francisco: Jossey-Bass Publishers, 1990).

52. Schorr, *Within Our Reach* ·

53. William E. Nothdurft, "Marketing Public Policy: Crafting the Product and Drafting the Message," *The Entrepreneurial Economy Review*, July/August 1988, vol.7, no.1 (published by the Corporation for Enterprise Development).

54. *Ibid.*

55. Jerry Wishrow, The Wishrow Group, Marblehead, Massachusetts.

ACADEMY SUPPORTERS

This Policy Guide was funded by the John D. and Catherine T. MacArthur Foundation. It reflects knowledge gained through CGPA's Policy Academy on Families and Children At-Risk. We wish to express our deepest appreciation to those who supported the Academy. They are:

    ARCO Foundation
    AT&T Foundation
    Ford Foundation
    Foundation for Child Development
    Irving Harris Trust
    Charles Stewart Mott Foundation
    U.S. Department of Health and Human Services
    U.S. Department of Labor
    United Way of Maryland

The Council also wishes to acknowledge the generous support of our Corporate Associates and of the nonprofit institutions that are Associate Members of the Council. Through their annual contributions, these organizations provide general support for the Council's research and membership services—funding our initial research on new issues, our technical assistance to states on strategic policy development and governance, and our foresight program.

Corporate Associates

    American Express
    Ameritech Foundation
    AT&T
    Atlantic Richfield Corporation
    Bell Atlantic Corporation
    BellSouth
    Burlington Northern
    General Electric Company
    Goldman Sachs
    Honeywell Incorporated
    Monsanto
    NYNEX Corporation
    Pacific Telesis Group
    Southwestern Bell Foundation
    3M Company

Associate Members

    The John F. Kennedy School of Government
      Harvard University
    The Port Authority of New York and New Jersey
    The Illinois Board of Education

ALSO PUBLISHED BY CGPA

Getting Results: A Guide for Government Accountability
    Jack A. Brizius and Michael D. Campbell

Creating Opportunity: Reducing Poverty Through Economic Development
    Hugh O'Neill

Out From Under: Policy Lessons From a Quarter Century of Wars on Poverty
    William E. Nothdurft and Barbara Dyer

Enhancing Adult Literacy: A Policy Guide
    Jack A. Brizius and Susan E. Foster

The Safety Net as Ladder: Transfer Payments for Economic Development
    Robert Friedman

On the Rebound: Helping Workers Cope With Plant Closings
    Terry F. Buss and Roger J. Vaughan

Preventing Teenage Pregnancy: A Public Policy Guide
    Susan E. Foster

The Wealth of States: Policies for a Dynamic Economy
    Roger Vaughan, Robert Pollard, and Barbara Dyer

Thinking Strategically: A Primer for Public Leaders
    Susan Walter and Pat Choate

The Game Plan: Governing With Foresight
    John D. Olsen and Douglas C. Eadie

Strategic Policy for the Nation's Governors: Organizing for Effective Policy
    Development and Implementation
    Lauren Cook, Ed.

Anticipating Tomorrow's Issues: A Handbook for Policymakers
Lauren Cook, B. Jack Osterholt, and Edward C. Riley, Jr.

OTHER SUGGESTED READINGS

Beyond Rhetoric, A New American Agenda for Children and Families
National Commission on Children (Washington, DC: 1991)

The Changing American Family and Public Policy
Andrew J. Cherlin, Ed. (Washington, DC: The Urban Institute Press, 1988)

Kids Count Data Book, State Profiles of Child Well-Being
Center for the Study of Social Policy (Washington DC: 1991)

Preparing Practitioners to Work with Infants, Toddlers, and Their Families: Issues and Recommendations for Policymakers
Emily Schrag Fenichel and Linda Eggbeer (Washington, DC: National Center for Clinical Infant Programs, 1990)

Programs to Strengthen Families
Yale University Bush Center In Child Development and Social Policy and *The Family Resource Coalition (Chicago: 1991)*

Raising Our Future: Families, Schools and Communities Joining Together
Heather Weiss (Cambridge, MA: Harvard Family Research Project, 1991)

Social Policy for Children and Families, A Review of Selected Reports
Deborah R. Both and Laurie Garduque, Ed. (Washington, DC: National Academy Press, 1989)

Thinking Collaboratively: Ten Questions and Answers to Help Policy Makers Improve Children's Services
Charles Bruner (Washington, DC: Education and Human Services Consortium, Institute for Educational Leadership, 1991)

The Unfinished Agenda: A New Vision for Child Development and Education
   Committee for Economic Development (New York: 1991)

What It Takes: Structuring Interagency Partnerships to Connect Children and
Families With Comprehensive Services
   *Atelia I. Melaville and Martin J. Blank (Washington, DC: Education
   and Human Services Consortium, Institute for Educational
   Leadership, 1991)*

Within Our Reach: Breaking the Cycle of Disadvantage
   Lisbeth Schorr (New York: Doubleday, 1988)